DIXIE
UNCUT
THE LOST INTERVIEW

DIXIE
UNCUT
THE LOST INTERVIEW

SPORT MEDIA
Trinity Mirror North West

Foreword by BRIAN LABONE

Published in Great Britain in 2005 by:
Trinity Mirror Sport Media,
PO Box 48, Old Hall Street,
Liverpool L69 3EB

Executive Editor: KEN ROGERS
Art Editor: RICK COOKE

ISBN 0-9546871-7-5

Printed and finished by Scotprint, Haddington, Scotland

Contents

Foreword

by Brian Labone

I felt privileged to know Dixie Dean, or Bill, as he preferred to be called.

His goalscoring record was incredible. But for all he achieved, he remained a down-to-earth fellow and a hell of a character. He was a lovely man and larger than life.

He had a great friend called Gordon Watson who played with him at Everton. I used to hear all these stories about Dixie but somehow I didn't think they could be quite true. But Gordon confirmed many of the tales.

My favourites related to Dixie having a few pints in the Winslow Hotel the night before a game and then go out and score three or four! He was a brilliant centre-forward and his feat of scoring 60 league goals in a season is definitely a record that is never going to be beaten.

When Dixie had to have his leg amputated in 1976, Gordon and I went to visit him at Birkenhead General Hospital. The staff told us that he had needed a major blood transfusion and we needed to tread softly. I remember Gordon and I tip-toeing into the room expecting to see him in a poorly state wired up to various tubes. But he was sat up watching the racing on a portable television with a bottle of beer at the side of his bed. He looked over at Gordon and myself and said: "That flaming Lester Piggott has just let me down again!"

I was with Dixie on his final day, March 1st, 1980. There was a special lunch before the derby at Goodison to launch the Liverpool and Everton annuals and Dixie, Bill Shankly and Bill Liddell were all there as well.

Shankly gave a lovely eulogy about Dixie. He spoke long and fondly about Dixie and then Dixie spoke about Shanks. Then we went on to the game and it came out that Dixie had died. It was a very sad end to the day.

I was extremely honoured to be one of the pallbearers who carried the coffin at his funeral over in Birkenhead. Maybe honoured is the wrong word because I was very sad that he had died. But there was me, Bob Latchford, Mick Lyons and Gordon West and it was a moving moment.

They have since put up a marvellous statue to Bill at the Stanley Park end of the ground and it is a fitting tribute. His birthday was January 22nd and mine is January 23rd. I walked by the statue when Everton played Charlton on January 22nd, 2005 and Bill's family had laid a lovely bouquet in blue-and-white.

This book gives an insight into Bill's character, his wonderful sense of humour and, perhaps most striking of all, his love of Everton.

Preface

On May 8, 1971, Merseyside's historic Football Echo launched a long-awaited football series that would run for an astonishing four and a half months.

The previous day, the Echo itself had highlighted the series with a general assessment of the career of Everton Football Club's most famous son, the legendary William Ralph "Dixie" Dean.

The great centre-forward's remarkable story, as told by the man himself, was intended to capture the imagination of Football Echo readers throughout the summer months and then carry them forward into a new season. To put it into time context, this was just a year after Everton's famous 1969/70 Championship victory – the era of Labone, Ball, Harvey, Kendall and the rest.

It was a bold piece of newspaper marketing to try and lock readers into the Dean story over such a long period, but the truth is that this was always going to be a sure-fire winner.

Dixie spent weeks reliving his glory days with Echo sports editor of the day Michael Charters who typed every single word (all 30,000 of them) on an old fashioned typewriter. They were then re-keyed into hot metal by an army of Echo typesetters, each sitting in front of monster Linotype machines that spat out text in molten lead in those pre-computer days when newspaper offices were more like factories than smart call centres.

Perhaps we shouldn't be surprised at the record-breaking timescale of the Dean series. After all, here was the greatest football record-breaker of all time, a real-life Roy of the Rovers whose 60 top-flight goals, plundered in season 1927-28, still stands as a figure that will never be beaten.

The Echo's library staff, with an astute sense of forward thinking, asked Charters for his original manuscript and filed it away in the newspaper archive along with the series' press cuttings. Here it lay, largely undisturbed and forgotten for over 20 years, until 1992 when one of Charters' successors, Ken Rogers, found it while researching "Goodison Glory " – the official Centenary history of Everton's famous stadium.

Rogers knew instinctively that one day the story of the immortal Dean would need to be retold and realised just how important the uncut, completely unedited Charters' manuscript was. He re-filed it in a locked store below the Echo building that also housed things like historic sports pictures and hand-written statistical books compiled by Echo sports writers for a century and more.

Another 13 years passed and then a routine Echo content meeting highlighted the fact that a significant date was looming linked with the 25th anniversary of Dixie's death. The great number nine passed away while watching an Everton-Liverpool derby at Goodison Park on March 1st, 1980. Rogers immediately thought about the Charters' manuscript.

Incredibly, he found it exactly where he had left it in that locked sports store. Alongside the 450 neatly typed pages that made up the 18-part series, he also found Charters' rough notes. Michael had clearly taped the interview and then transcribed it word for word, including questions and answers. These yellowing pages give us a real feel for how his interviews with Dixie unfolded.

As Dean himself begins to revel in his personal memories, a remarkable story unfolds that pulls no punches and provides a fascinating insight into the life of a leading professional footballer in those days when players were slaves to a maximum wage and clubs were all-powerful in every sense.

It is this story "Dixie Uncut – The Lost Interview" that is told here.

Rogers, now Executive Editor of the Trinity Mirror Sport Media Magazine Unit based within the Echo building, sought and received the full support of Echo Editor Mark Dickinson to turn the Dean manuscript into an anniversary book.

A famous Evertonian battle song is "If You Know Your History." This publication will help all true Blues, young and old, to grasp the full amazing story of the greatest of them all – William Ralph "Dixie" Dean.

There's no debate...
Dean simply was the greatest
Introduction by Ken Rogers

William Ralph "Dixie" Dean reigns supreme as the greatest Everton player of all time.

That's a bold statement when you consider the legendary status of a club whose fans revel in a proud and illustrious history.

Dean remains the King of Goodison Park for many reasons. His record of having scored 60 top-flight League goals in season 1927-28 still stands and will never be beaten. This alone confirms his position as the brightest star in Everton's royal blue heaven.

But Dean was more than a goal machine and the most prolific centre-forward of all time.

Fundamentally he was an Evertonian. He loved the Mersey Blues and that passion captured the imagination of the people who idolised him. When you talk about the People's Club, here was the definitive man of the people.

Dean had no side to him. For a spell, he lived in a club house in the shadow of the ground. One of his locals would have been the Winslow pub facing the club's main entrance. Fittingly, the pub still carries his image on the sign that swings above the front door. At this time, Dixie would walk the 50 yards or so to the game, exchanging jokes, stories and gossip along the way as he made his way through the matchday throng.

There was no pomposity about him. Here was a man who was as down to earth as they come. He was a boy when he arrived from Tranmere. He was a man when he left Everton. The bit in between was the stuff of folklore.

I was not lucky enough to see Dean play. I probably saw him kick-off a charity game at some unglamorous venue like South Liverpool's tiny (and now demolished) Holly Park ground in the late Sixties as I began my journalistic football career covering matches in the old Northern Premier League.

But I count myself one of the luckiest people in the world because I got to know Dixie, or Bill as he preferred to be called, as the years unfolded. I would ultimately have the honour of staging and sustaining the Liverpool Echo's annual Dixie Dean Memorial Award dinner as sports editor of the Liverpool Echo.

But amongst my favourite memories of the great man were priceless hours spent alone with him in the city centre Littlewoods garage/supply stores near Ranelagh Street where he worked in his latter years, having been given what seemed to me to be a fairly menial job by John Moores – the power behind the throne at Everton in the Sixties and Seventies.

That's certainly not how Bill Dean saw it. Working class heroes still have to make a living.

I was a young sports editor of the old Liverpool Weekly News at that time, based in Bold Street. When I found out that an Everton legend and my all-time sporting hero was working round the corner, I wasted no time in introducing myself and taking copious notes as he happily regaled me with stories about his playing days.

We would sit in a tiny hut that stood within the garage and I would listen to his fascinating stories about that golden era when he scored hat-tricks for fun en-route to becoming a football immortal.

I found it hard to understand how such an icon had ended up pushing a trolley and moving goods around in this most uninspiring and depressing of places, but Dean was not embarrassed. Far from it, he was proud to be working – being a man of the Twenties and Thirties when the great depression put millions out of work and on the streets.

Modern players earn more in a week than Dean probably earned in all of his time at Everton. But money can't buy you a passport into Football's Hall of Fame. Only genius can do that – and Dean was the definitive matchwinner who captured the hearts and minds of fans all over the country.

To Evertonians he was a god. To opponents he was Attila The Hun in spring-heeled football boots. He could shoot accurately, but his main strength was an ability to destroy opponents with his towering ability in the air.

And here is where the folklore merges with the fact. As a boy in the Fifties, my father and grandfather would tell me that Dean could head the ball the length of the field. Now I knew it was physically impossible, but then so was the logic of Father Christmas coming down the chimney to deliver my Christmas presents.

What they were really saying was that his unique aerial prowess qualified him for a pilot's licence. This area of his game was simply unmatchable in an era of giants.

These were the times when men were prepared to put their heads in the way of a piece of leather that, on a wet day, would weigh as much as a cannonball.

No wonder a scientific study years later indicated that Alzheimer's Disease could be brought on by the repetitive heading of these football weapons of mass destruction. It is no coincidence that many old footballers suffered from memory loss in later life.

Dean, despite once sustaining major head injuries following a motor cycle accident, never shied away from thundering crosses fired in from right or left or a launched defensive clearance that would soar so high it would come down with snow on it.

He was the undisputed 'King of The Air' in an age of magnificent number nines and those folklore comments were simply aimed at emphasising the point.

In 1992 I had the honour of being asked to write the Official Centenary History of Goodison Park, the end game of which was the first edition of Goodison Glory.

Naturally, Dean would dominate a series of chapters and I decided to find out the facts about just how good he was by researching a whole season of match reports in the Football Echo.

What came through was astonishing. Sometimes your memory can play tricks and you exaggerate the strengths and qualities of the heroes you have seen. That's what folklore is all about. But in the case of Dixie, he was actually better than I ever imagined. In almost every paragraph of every match report, he was exerting a massive influence.

It was clear he was as strong as an ox. He could shoot with fearsome accuracy with both feet. He was as brave as they come when fending off the assassins who marauded as defenders in those days.

He had this incredible knack of jumping at the right time to outfox his marker before directing a header in any direction. His teammates would launch balls up and the wingers would run beyond their captain. Dean would glance balls left and right or he would loop them over defenders into space. Then he would be on the move, anticipating the pinpoint cross that would come from outstanding wide players like Ted Critchley, Alec Troup, Jimmy Stein and Albert Geldard.

You can imagine the anticipation inside a packed Goodison when this regular tactical ploy unfolded and Dean turned and roared towards the edge of the box. A momentary silence would descend as every fan took a deep breath, mesmerised and soaking up this scene as if caught up in a slow motion replay. Then all hell would let loose as every muscle and sinew exploded as the winger's cross looped into the box.

Dean would fly though the air with his football radar locked firmly onto the target and another goal would be in the bag. In my imagination, every shot or header would burst through the back of the net, forcing the first 20 rows of fans to duck before the ball demolished a steel crash barrier with its sheer force. Okay, now I'm back into the realms of my father's Dixie folklore, but you get the picture.

And let me be clear. When I said that I'd studied all of those archive editions of the Football Echo to clarify Dean's real impact on all things Everton, I was not exaggerating. He was an all-dominating force and so my early declaration that he was truly 'the greatest' is unquestionable.

If I was given one trip in a football time machine to watch a single moment of action in any era, I would set the dial for that mind-blowing day at Goodison Park on May 3rd, 1928 when Dean, with one of Arsenal's greatest ever teams in opposition, stood on the brink of immortality with 57 goals already in the bag and George Camsell's all-time scoring record in his sights.

That he scored a sensational hat-trick in a 3-3 draw in front of a crowd of 48,715 delirious supporters to set a new benchmark is astounding. That he probably celebrated with those fans in the pub over the road minutes after the final whistle is all part of the folklore. How many pints did Dixie put away that night? I'm not sure, but probably that also still stands as a record that will never be beaten!

I've been lucky enough to see many great Everton moments. The 1963 title clinching day against Fulham when another treble, struck by the great Roy Vernon, raised the Goodison roof. The 1970 title-winning moment against West Brom when 58,523 packed into Goodison to see Colin Harvey and Alan Whittle put the Blues into an unassailable position with two games still to play.

I covered Everton for the Echo throughout the remarkable Eighties, the most successful era in the history of the club. I saw Bayern battered into submission and Rapid Vienna destroyed. I saw the taming of Manchester United at Wembley in 1995 and witnessed those Nineties nailbiters against

Wimbledon and Coventry. These were all days fans would proudly like to declare: "I was there."

But I suspect all of us would opt for Dixie's finest hour as our Time Machine destination.

Bill Shankly said of the Everton legend: "Dixie was the greatest centre-forward there will ever be. His record of goalscoring is the most amazing thing under the sun."

That Everton's arch-rival crossed the Park from Anfield to become such an enthusiastic and willing member of the prestigious panel of judges that selected the early winners of the Echo's Dixie Dean Memorial Award says everything about Everton's Greatest.

One of the saddest moments of my life came in October, 1991, when I travelled to Glasgow for the Echo to report on the sale of Dean's medal collection (his 1933 FA Cup winning medal apart). The set included the Holy Grail of football, the 1928 League Championship medal that was claimed on the back of those 60 legendary goals. There was also a baseball medal in the collection, highlighting Dixie's all-round sporting prowess.

Down the years I had seen those medals many times in the presence of the great man himself and later his proud daughter Barbara who became their custodian following Bill's death on March 1st, 1980. Ironically, he passed away during a Merseyside derby clash.

It was an honour to hold each and every one of those medals and feel the force of past glory days. It was tragic that the collection could not have been kept intact in the only place where it deserved to be – Dean's beloved Goodison where he made history and where he died. Imagine what a tourist attraction those medals would have become.

I watched helplessly as the hammer came down time and again. The collection was taken apart by a string of individuals and spread far and wide.

There is no doubt in my mind that Everton could have secured the entire collection at that time for a figure in the region of ten to fifteen thousand pounds. Ultimately, a private collector paid £9,350 for the 1928 title medal alone.

My media colleague John Keith who wrote "Dixie Dean – The Inside Story Of A Football Icon" made a very pertinent point when he pointed out that £9,350 was more than three times what Everton had paid Tranmere for Dean. But in true terms the medal was simply priceless from an Everton standpoint.

Dean's 1931-32 Championship medal went for £3,520 and his 1932 FA

Charity Shield medal for slightly less at £3,300. A 1926-27 international medal went under the hammer for £3,080 and his 1928 FA Charity Shield medal for £2,420.

I desperately wanted to bid for one of the minor medals, just to have something that belonged to my all-time hero, but throughout the auction I was on the phone to the Echo, dictating the story for that night's edition as the sale unfolded.

Thankfully, Derek Johnson – Everton's Commercial Manager at the time – managed to secure a couple of medals for the Goodison collection within the fairly tight cash restraints that were imposed on him. Derek had tried hard to secure a bolder remit from the Goodison hierarchy.

In my view, the decision not to buy Dean's collection outright was short-sighted bordering on catastrophic.

In March, 2001, Bill Kenwright turned all of that around when he ensured that a record £18,212 was paid, this time at a Christie's auction in London, for Dean's 1933 FA Cup winning medal which had a reserve price of £8,000 placed on it by Dean's son Geoff. Everton's majority shareholder had declared that a medal belonging to Everton's greatest ever player was never going anywhere else but Goodison Park.

It sits proudly within the collection in the Dixie Dean Lounge today for all to see – a testament to a football giant. Thank god Bill Kenwright's Everton heart understood the importance of that piece of silverware to all Blues.

Fittingly, the Echo's Dixie Dean Memorial Award continues to be presented at an annual ceremony. Meanwhile the giant Dean Statue stands proudly at the gateway to Goodison, permanently festooned with flowers and often used these days by Evertonians to remember other royal blue members of their family who might have died.

A song-writing friend of mine, Gerry Markey, decided to pen a tribute to the great Everton number nine with a view to it being sung each year at the Dean Memorial Award. Ironically, Gerry is a Liverpudlian, but that only serves to make his words even more poignant. They highlight the fact that Dean commanded the total respect across the great divide.

I print the opening words to Gerry's "Ballad Of Dixie Dean" with the memory in my mind of an evening sitting next to Dixie's daughter Barbara and granddaughter Melanie when the song was first played in public. Their tears were for a dad and a granddad they loved and missed. Our tears were for a man who was a soccer superstar before the phrase was invented . . .

THE BALLAD OF DIXIE DEAN by GERRY MARKEY

On the banks of the River Mersey, It was morning in the street
A boy in a football jersey, Is playing music with his feet
He is bound for greater glory, Than the north end has ever seen
And generations will tell the story, Of the legendary Dixie Dean

He was born on the north side, In the age of the First World War
He was a railway worker's boy child , In an age when they had nothing at all
He was a hunter in a frozen field, In search of a leather caseball
And little did we know, He'd be the greatest of them all

So hello Dixie Dean You are the greatest centre-forward ever seen
Oh what a pleasure it must have been, Just to see you play
You are the legend of 60 goals, In one League season all told
The Prince of St. Domingo Road, And Liverpool Bay

Chapter One

Everton trainer slept in my room for three nights to get me fit for 60 goal record

I know a lot has been written about the time I broke the League record by scoring 60 goals in the 1927-28 season. But I want to start by telling you a story about what happened before the match against Arsenal on the last day of the season when I scored the three goals I needed for the record. I don't think this story has ever been told before because it was kept a close secret at the time.

You see, I nearly didn't play against Arsenal at all. And if it hadn't been for old Harry Cooke I wouldn't have played at all.

Harry was the trainer at Everton in all my years there and he was a great character. His birthday was the same day as mine, 22nd January, and he was like a father to me.

The position was this. George Camsell had set the League scoring record at 59 in the season before, but that was in the Second Division.

With two games to go I had scored 53 in 37 League games, so I wanted seven goals from the last two matches to beat George's record.

The first of these two games was at Burnley on the Wednesday of the last week of the season. I got four that day all before half-time, and I was particularly pleased because I was playing against Big Jack Hill, the England centre-half in those days, and a particular pal of mine.

He was reckoned the best in the business then, but any rate, I got four against Big Jack and he rubbed his face on the ground when the fourth one went in.

I didn't do anything in the second half because I pulled a thigh muscle badly, and I was in some pain. Old Harry Cooke was shaking when he found out about it and so was I.

Harry was really worried that I wouldn't be able to play against Arsenal, so when we got back from Burnley that night, he came with me to my home in Alderley Avenue, Birkenhead.

He wanted to put hot plasters on my leg to get the muscle right. You're supposed to leave these plasters on pretty hot for about ten or twelve hours, but Harry wasn't content with that.

He wanted to change them every two hours so that the heat from the plasters would really work.

So I went to bed and he sat in a chair in my bedroom and woke me up every two hours so that he could put a fresh plaster on.

He did this for three nights on the run – the Wednesday, Thursday and Friday nights before the Arsenal game. He put hot towels on as well, and without him I'd never have played that day and never broken that record.

What we used to do was that in the morning I'd run him to his home in Wallasey before we went over to Goodison for more treatment.

I didn't know how he'd stuck it for three nights on end without much sleep, but he told me he used to try and get a few hours each afternoon before he came back to my home in Birkenhead to start putting on the plasters all over again.

All the lads at Everton would do anything for Harry and he was a wonderful man to me.

Anyway, he got me fit for the Arsenal match and I got the three goals I needed to set up a new record.

I remember the goals well. The first was a penalty. I was going through with the ball and got to about the penalty spot when the goalkeeper pulled my legs from under me.

So that was a penalty and I scored. The second goal was just before half-time. I hit it with my right foot and the ball went in the far corner.

Things tightened up a bit after that with the Arsenal defence being so good. It wasn't until about four minutes from the end that we got a corner kick on the left.

Alec Troup took the kick. He was so precise with these corners that he could have laid the ball on one of the hairs on my head. Any rate he sent over this beautiful corner kick and that sailed in. I just butted the ball in. The crowd invaded the pitch and I got more whiskers on my face from the Scotland Road lads than Soft Joe.

You see, these lads swarmed all round me, some of them rubbing their faces against mine and a lot of them hadn't shaved that day.

When they got the ground cleared the game started again, but there wasn't much longer to play. A couple of minutes from the end I went up to the referee and said: "I'll be shooting off in a minute. You don't mind do you?"

He said: "I don't blame you, Dean." So I got off before I got another attack of the whiskers.

It's a funny thing but I didn't get anything from Everton for breaking the scoring record – no celebration or presents or anything.

But the Supporters Club was very good. They gave me a big shield and on it was a record of each one of the 60 goals I'd scored showing the grounds I'd scored them on.

It's a beautiful thing and I treasure it. I've shown it around a lot to people and I'm very proud of it.

I suppose Everton couldn't give me anything special unless they applied to the League. If they had given it to me they'd have had to give it to the others as well.

Chapter Two

The day I scored 12 before dinner and 18 in one day

My football life in Merseyside brought me every football honour possible. I was born on January 22nd, 1907, at 313 Laird Street, Birkenhead, in the North end of the town.

My father was an engine driver with Wirral Railways and I had six sisters.

Being an only boy I suppose I was mainly in the way at home and used to be a bit of a nuisance, so I used to go and live away from home as a boy.

One of the places I lived was in the Albert Industrial School near my home.

I went to Laird Street Council School and left there when I was fourteen. Altogether I played for the school team for four years and also two years with the Birkenhead Boys team - the town team.

I was always mad about playing football and Everton was always the team that I followed from my first early memories of being interested in the game.

I would be about eight or nine years old when I can remember life, even as a boy, being dominated by football. I was so keen that I used to go and train by myself.

There was an old chapel in the North end of Birkenhead and I used to kick a ball against the chapel wall, and keep running up and down playing the ball backwards and forwards against the wall.

But one of the greatest things I can remember was the chapel roof. It helped to give me a good start with the old heading trick.

I chalked the outline of a goal on the chapel wall and then threw the ball onto the roof.

I'd wait for it to come down and then I'd move in to head it against the wall between the goal posts. Looking back, I am sure this helped me with my heading, but I must say that I was always good at heading. It was a natural gift.

I was twelve when I first played for Birkenhead Boys, at centre-forward. We played Liverpool at Tranmere Rovers' ground and they beat us 6-1.

My father had promised to give me a shilling for every goal I scored, and that represented a fortune to a boy in those days after the First World War.

But Liverpool gave us a real hammering that day and when I wasn't getting any goals I went to full-back to try and stop Liverpool scoring. As a matter of fact, I did score – an own goal.

That's more than I ever did during my time with Everton. I wouldn't have liked to have done that against them at Anfield or Goodison. As a matter of fact, although I scored a goal, my father refused to pay me the shilling.

In those days there was no such thing as a Cheshire team for schoolboys, but there were Boys' International matches. I was picked to play in an England trial, but lost the chance through splitting a knee-cap in a match – just the first of a lot of injuries I had in my career.

I was off for quite a time with that injury, but played for two years for Birkenhead Boys and I can remember that I just couldn't play enough football to satisfy me. I remember one day particularly because I scored eighteen goals in one day.

I was thirteen at the time. There was a Birkenhead Boys trial at Prenton Playing Fields in the morning starting at about nine o'clock. I scored six goals in the match and then me and the rest of the lads in the team got on our bikes and dashed down to Birkenhead Park to play another match starting at eleven o'clock.

I scored another six goals for them and then in the afternoon played for a team called Melville and scored another six.

So that was eighteen in three games, so I wasn't too surprised when I got sixty in a season for Everton.

I always had a lust for scoring goals, even as a schoolboy. Once more, I practised hard at it, because I was no use whatsoever as a scholar at school.

I could just about write a bit, but I couldn't put two and two together and spent all my time playing football.

I used to sag school quite a lot. I don't know if you understand what sag means these days, but it means staying away from school, playing truant.

The old headmaster used to get onto me and promised me a good hiding if I stayed away from school, and one day I got really scared.

That afternoon all the boys were called into the main hall and when we got there, there was a man from the Education Offices with the headmaster. He said: "William Ralph Dean come forward."

I thought: "This is it, they are going to give me the stick in front of everyone."

But it turned out that the man from the Education Office was there to present me with a medal for playing with Birkenhead Boys – the first medal I ever received, and I still have it to this day.

So it turned out to be one of the best days I had at school. I asked the teacher if I could slip home and show the medal to my mother. He let me go and I stayed away for three days just to celebrate, but they were great times.

Apart from myself, there was one other boy in that Birkenhead team who turned professional. That was Ellis Rimmer, the outside-left. He was a very good player and he following me to Tranmere and from there he was transferred to Sheffield Wednesday.

He won practically the same honours as I did - a League Championship medal, a Cup medal and played for England. He also scored in every round of the FA Cup.

Chapter Three

Tranmere promised me £300 to sign for Everton, but they forgot one of the noughts

After leaving school at fourteen and the three years before I joined my first professional club, Tranmere Rovers, the most vivid memories I have are of playing football as often as I could.

Of course, I got a job through my father's help on the Wirral Railways. I was an apprentice fitter and the first suit I ever owned was a boiler suit to wear at work.

We didn't have much money in those days, so my working suit was my first long trousers as a fourteen year old.

I left school on Friday and started work the following Monday. It was shift work, three shifts in the twenty-four hours and the other two apprentices with me didn't like the night shift.

I did because it gave me more time during the day to play football. The Wirral Railways ground was alongside where I worked and I used to nip over the railings and play.

I played for the Railways' team, mainly at centre forward, but I also used to have a go at other forward positions when the team thought they'd found another good centre forward.

I also used to play for a team called Pensby United in the Wirral Combination. They had a good side in those days.

It was while I was playing for Pensby that a Tranmere Rovers scout called "Dump" Lee asked me if I would like to join Tranmere.

I'd be just seventeen then and I went along to see Bert Cook, the Tranmere Secretary-Manager.

"Dump" Lee had recommended me pretty strongly, I gather, and Cook signed me quickly and gave me £4-5s-0d a week (£4.25p). This was a big difference to the wages I was on as an apprentice fitter. That was about twelve shillings (60p). When I signed season 1923-24 was practically finished and I only played in a couple of games.

But the next season I went straight into the first team and stayed there. Some of the best known players in the side were Stan Sears, Jackson, Frank Cheetham, who was a schoolteacher, Fred Halstead, Cartman, Jimmy Morgan and Jackie Brown, the Irish international. In that season, 1924-25, I played twenty-seven games for Tranmere and scored twenty-seven goals. They put up my pay to £5 and in those days it was a lot of money.

Mind you, we didn't get paid in the summer. Bert Cook reckoned they didn't pay summer money, so in the summer I was with Tranmere I had to go out and find myself another job.

There was a milk shop next door to where I lived in Laird Street, so I got a job with them delivering milk. We used to collect the milk at five in the morning and then deliver it, so that kept me going during the close season.

The trainer at Tranmere used to be all on physical fitness. We did about an hour's shooting in a week and that was the only time we saw a ball between matches. It was only when I got to Everton that I found all the different ideas about training.

I was the youngest in the Tranmere team and I believed in training.

A typical day's work would be a ten mile run from Prenton Park around towards Upton and back.

I did that two mornings a week and then in the afternoon we would do a few laps, sprints and some exercises.

As I said, I always had this gift for scoring goals and I averaged one a match when I was at Tranmere. I began to be noted by senior clubs.

The first one ever to approach me was Newcastle United. We had been playing at Ashington when the Newcastle trainer, who had been watching, me asked if I would like to join Newcastle.

I told him no. Then Aston Villa and Arsenal tried the same approach and I gave them the same answer.

You see, I was just waiting for one club to come for me and that was Everton.

They were the only club I ever wanted to play for. I wouldn't have gone to Liverpool, only Everton.

This began from my schooldays. I only used to look for the result of one team in the Echo on a Saturday and that was Everton.

I didn't care if Liverpool were licked 10-0. That wouldn't affect me at all.

If Everton won, that was fine. If they lost, well, it was a bad day.

I had been to the pictures one afternoon and when I got home there was my father and mother with Bert Cook. As soon as I saw Cook's face I knew something had happened and he said to me: "Would you like to play for Everton?"

Well, of course, that was it. We went to the Woodside Hotel at Birkenhead and there we met Mr. Tom McIntosh, the Everton secretary.

They didn't have a manager in those days and he was in charge. I didn't even bother to discuss terms with him. I told him: "I'll take what you give me, because Everton is where I want to go."

Bert Cook had promised my parents that I'd get £300 from Tranmere when I signed for Everton. He said it would be a good start for me in life and they thought it was very good.

A fortnight after I'd signed for Everton, I went to Tranmere to get the cheque. He handed it to me and I said to him: "You've missed an '0' off this."

He said, "What do you mean?" I said: "That cheque says £30 instead of £300. You've missed an '0' off."

He said, "I'm sorry, Billy, that's all the League will allow you." But I told him that I was not going to take the cheque because he had promised my parents this money while I was there. I went to see Mr. John McKenna, who was Chairman of Liverpool and also President of the Football League.

I explained to him what had happened and he said: "If you'd have come to me before you signed the transfer forms, I could have helped you. I can't help you now you've signed and that's the answer." So that was the end of that and I never got my £300.

Anyway, I had signed for the club I wanted to join above all others, and that was the main thing. Everton paid Tranmere £3,000 and they got that back exactly from Notts. County when they transferred me to that club thirteen years later almost to the day.

Chapter Four

Heading – The real secret

My wages went up by £1 from £5 to £6 when I joined Everton on March 16, 1925. I was eighteen and I went straight into the first team.

There were a lot of experienced players, many of them internationals, at Goodison Park and I was very much the young boy in what I suppose would be an old team.

It was near the end of the season and I remember that there were a couple of centre forwards around at that time - Jack Cock, an international, and Jimmy Broad.

Everton sold both of them before the end of next season. Cock went to Millwall and Broad to Stoke.

Everton hadn't done much for years. In fact, I don't think they had done anything since they won the Cup in 1906. One of the best-known men in the side when I joined them was Sammy Chedgzoy. He was the England outside right and proved a real daddy to me in helping me to settle down at Goodison Park. Then there was Bobby Irvine, the Irish international inside right. He was very good. He was better than Georgie Best at dribbling the ball. I've seen him bring it the length of the field beating man after man.

On the left wing was little Alex Troup. He was a Scottish international and I had a lot to thank him for because he was such a great man in crossing the ball from the wing.

The team was full of Scottish men in those days – the left backs, MacDonald and Wright and also Billy Brown and Hunter Hart.

Both Chedgzoy and Troup helped me a great deal. Sammy used to say to me: "When you see me going down the wing and keeping to the line, I want you to go to the far corner of the penalty area. That will give you room to run in there and you will find these crosses coming over for you."

And that's exactly what they did – Alex Troup as well. He was even more accurate than Sammy, and used to hit them harder.

It's much better for a centre forward to be able to head a fast moving centre. I could either head it directly or flick it on to someone else, and Troup's centres were made to order.

In those days, of course, we played with the old type leather ball which got very heavy in wet weather. But I never had any trouble heading a heavy ball.

The secret of heading a ball is to catch it on your forehead. If you get it on top of your head it will knock you daft in no time.

I saw quite a few players knocked unconscious after heading a ball wrongly. I remember playing in an England trial game with the Arsenal centre forward, Tom Parker. He went up for a ball, headed it and was taken to hospital with concussion. He was out of the game for six weeks.

The great thing is anticipating the ball coming over and catching it with your forehead. I suppose I had an insight for going up at the right time.

I was not as tall as many of the centre halves I played against. I was about 5'11" and a lot of them were around 6'2." But I never had any difficulty in beating them in the air.

It wasn't a case of leaping higher than they could. It was just a matter of going up at the right moment. You knew that he was going to miss the ball because he'd probably be coming down as I was going up.

In those days a club could apply to the League to increase your wages by £1, and as soon as I started getting a few goals for Everton, my wages went up from £6 to £7, and shortly after £8. It was only that much all the time I was at Everton and I also got a £6 a week summer wage.

I had a few games in the reserves as well in the few weeks immediately after I'd joined Everton. But at the start of the next season, 1926-27, I went straight into the first team and stayed there.

I remember we didn't have a good season. We didn't do anything. We were just an ordinary struggling team.

They hadn't brought any new players except myself, so we kicked of with the same old crowd, but before the end of the season they got rid of a few because they used to have a lot of professional staff at Everton in those days, more than forty players.

I remember very well my first game for Everton in March 1925. It was at Arsenal and we lost 3-1.

I thought I scored a goal that day – a good one. The ball went into the side of the net and the goalkeeper grabbed it as it went over the line and threw it up the field quickly. So the referee decided it hadn't been in the net and disallowed it.

I scored that "goal" with my head but in the next game, against Aston Villa, at home, I did score my first goal for Everton – again with my head.

Playing at Goodison Park for a First Division club, on a great ground, was what I had always wanted above everything else. But it didn't affect me in any way. I didn't seem to have any nerves at all.

Even now, I can remember well my first game for Everton. The ball was played down to Alex Troup and he took it down the line almost to the corner flag.

I had watched him doing this in training during practice games so I knew just what position to take up for a centre.

He sent over the beautiful cross and that was that -– I just flicked it with my head and the goalkeeper had no chance.

The Everton crowd went mad, cheering and shouting. It was a wonderful moment and I'll never forget it.

Chapter Five

Crash nearly ended my career at 19

Although I've always preferred to be known by my Christian name of Billy, I've had this nickname of Dixie since I was a schoolboy and it has always lived with me.

I think the Everton crowd started to shout "Give it to Dixie" at the beginning of the 26-27 season. In the previous season I had shown them that I had the potential to score a lot of goals and they took up this cry, which stayed with me throughout my football career. There have been a lot of stories about how I got the nickname. One of them was that it had been given to me by my sister when she was a baby learning to talk, but that's not so.

The truth of it is that I was always very dark-skinned and as a youngster had a mop of black curls.

So I got this nickname (linked with the American South) at school and it has been with me ever since.

In the close season, before the start of the 26-27 season, I had an accident on a motor bike which I thought might have ended my career. I was only nineteen so you can guess how I felt.

I was riding my motorbike through Holywell and I had a girlfriend on the pillion.

A chap driving a car cut in and then dropped back and then suddenly cut in again coming towards me. I had the choice of either going into the car or going down the mountain so I went right through the windscreen of the car. But before the crash I was able to turn round and push the girl off the bike. She only damaged her ankle, fortunately, but I fractured my skull, broke a cheekbone and fractured my jaw in two places.

I woke up in the workhouse in Holywell with my jaw in splints. Apparently they didn't have a hospital there at that time so the only place they could put me was in the workhouse.

Soon afterwards Everton arranged to transfer me to a nursing home in West Derby. But I was in hospital for five months altogether.

Towards the end of my stay in the nursing home, Tom McIntosh, the Everton secretary, came to see me and as it happened I was climbing a tree in the hospital grounds knocking apples down for the nurses to catch. He said to me: "If you're well enough to do that, you can come back and play football." So that's what I did.

Because I'd been in hospital for so long I missed a lot of matches at the start of the 26-27 season. My first match back was in a Central League game at Huddersfield in October 1926. A special train-load of fans went through to Huddersfield to watch me play, because it had been thought at one time that I'd never play again.

 Old Harry Cooke was worried about what would happen when I first headed the ball. He told Teddy Critchley, our outside right that day, to try to try to get over a good centre to me early in the game so that I could head it.

Harry told me that if I felt any pain from my head after heading the ball I was to come off right away.

I remember it was a very heavy day so naturally we were all worried about what was going to happen when I headed the ball. After about a quarter of an hour over came the ball from Teddy Critchley. I thought to myself, "Here goes", and I went up to head it.

The ball flew into the net. I shook my head and I could see Harry Cooke on the line thinking something was wrong as I did so. They started to call me off but I shouted that there was nothing wrong.

In those days you got £1 bonus for winning a reserve game, and I was a goal up towards £1 so I stayed on. We won 2-0 and I've never felt anything wrong as a result of that accident ever since.

As a matter of fact, I think the skull fracture knitted twice as hard, so they tell me, and it considerably helped me with the old heading trick.

I could head a ball anywhere and anyway and I never got a pain or an ache or anything.

Before talking about the remainder of that 26-27 season, I must say that I found the training at Everton very different from that at Tranmere, which was a bit slack I must say.

For one thing, we had to sign the book when we came in each morning and that was very different to what I'd been used to.

We only went in on Monday morning if we'd had any injuries from the previous match and then we'd have treatment and tests.

Tuesday would be a full day's training. There would be road work in the morning, back to the ground for lunch and a bath and then more training for a couple of hours in the afternoon.

Wednesday would be another full day training and Thursday as well, but sometimes on a Wednesday afternoon, the lads who liked a game of golf would be given time off to play.

Everton had a marvellous gymnasium on an old practice ground behind the stand. It had everything, it was the last word. We could go in there any time we liked and practically every Friday we'd round off our weekly training with some sprints before perhaps going off to an away match.

We didn't practice moves like they do these days. The funniest thing that ever happened in those days about practising in training was at Arsenal. The manager, Herbert Chapman, set up a table like a football ground and started to move dominoes about while telling the players "I want you to go so-and-so and you go over there", moving the dominoes about as he was speaking.

Alex James walked in one day as he was doing this, took off his hat, and threw it on the table knocking all the dominoes all over the place. He said: "Yes, and that's what the other defence will be doing to us at the same time." So that was the end of practising using a board.

Chapter Six

60 goals – and 40 came from Troup's centres

At the start of season 26-27, we played two away games, one at Portsmouth and the other at Sunderland, and we won both 3-0. It looked as though we were going to have a really good season.

But it didn't turnout that way. I managed to score about forty goals that season but we finished about half way.

Sammy Chedgzoy had left us by then. He went during the summer to live in Canada and Everton didn't buy any new players for that season.

The great teams in that season were Newcastle, who won the title, and Arsenal. But I felt that I was picking up experience all the time and there were signs that the Everton side could develop into a great one.

Some of the great players of that time – people I played against – were Alex James and Joe Hulme of Arsenal, Willie Smith, the Huddersfield outside left, Big Jack Hill, the Burnley centre half, Joe Smith and David Jack of Bolton and Charlie Buchan of Sunderland and later Arsenal.

We at Everton also had one of the really great players of the time – Warney Creswell. Although many people think I could only score goals with my head, I got most of them with my feet. I developed this when I was at Tranmere when I scored twenty-seven in twenty-seven games.

The lads there used to tell me that if I carried on dribbling down the field, I'd get kicked up in the air.

But being young, I took no notice until one day we were playing against Rochdale.

I scored two goals by dribbling the ball forward and shooting and as I was coming back up the field this Rochdale fellow said to me: "Thy'll get no more bloody goals today."

I said: "You're too fat and old, what are you talking about?" But he was right. The next time I tried to dribble past him he kicked me. I got no more goals and I finished up in hospital for an operation. He was a good tipster that fellow.

I felt great at the start of the 27-28 season, which was to end with Everton winning the Championship and me breaking the scoring record. The team had changed a great deal from the previous season. In goal it was usually Ted Taylor with Creswell and O'Donnell at full back. The half back line was Kelly, Hart and Virr and in attack there was Ted Critchley, Dick Forshaw or George Martin, myself, Kennedy or Weldon, and Troup. We played the W formation. The wing players attacked and so did the inside forwards. As the wingers took the ball down the flanks, the other two would move forward and take up position behind me.

This was the Everton speciality. My job was not only to get goals but also to head centres from Critchley and Troup back to the inside forwards.

There were many times when they could almost walk the ball in the net. I'd be on one side of the goal when the centre came over and the other team would be expecting me to head it towards to the goal, but I would head it across the penalty area and one of these lads could simply walk it in.

It was a good all round team that year and little Alex Troup was a real smasher. He was only about 5'3" tall and one of his shoulder blades used to come out while he was playing. Old Harry Cooke used to take him down to the dressing room when the shoulder came out of place, jerk it back and the shoulder would come right again. Out of these sixty goals I scored this season I must have scored forty from centres by Troup, most of them with my head.

I can still remember some of the games and some of the goals I scored that season, in addition to the three I got in the last match against Arsenal, which I have already mentioned in the first chapter.

There was one game at Leicester where I had been pulled up a few times for offside. So I went over all nasty-like and said to the referee: "About this offside lark. Would you mind watching where I am when the ball's kicked and where I am when I head it."

He said he would. A free kick was taken and I was onside by about two yards. When the ball was in the air I went running ahead because I'd got an idea where the ball was going.

I reached the ball, put it in the net, and there were all the Leicester players appealing for offside. But the referee said: "No, not this time."

There was another goal at Aston Villa and I always think it was the sun gave it me that day. It was a beautiful day, sun shining brightly and the ball was coming right up the middle.

I was going to run onto this ball, trap it and try to take it forwards, but at that moment I saw a shadow on my right pass me. It was the shadow of Biddelston in the Villa goal. He had run out to try to catch the ball before I reached it, but when I saw his shadow go past me, I jumped up, back-headed the ball and it dropped into the net. I was just on the edge of the penalty area when I did it.

I only played in thirty-nine League games that season and scored sixty goals. In many of those matches I scored two and three, but the most I ever scored in a game that season was five. I scored them all before half time against Sunderland.

The Sunderland goalkeeper was a very sporting kind and I knew him well. We used to have a £1 bet every time we played each other that I would score against him, so I didn't have any trouble that afternoon in collecting my bet after beating him five times.

Chapter Seven

I silence Hampden Park with a double – and the amateurs at the FA suggest I didn't play well

Just before the season in which I broke the scoring record, I won my first cap. It was against Wales at Wrexham and we drew 3-3 and I managed to score two.

That was in February 1927, and I can remember quite a few of the players in the England team that day.

Brown of Sheffield Wednesday was in goal, Jimmy Seddon of Bolton was the centre half, and Willis Edwards was one of the wing halves.

I also played against Scotland at Hampden Park that season and that was one of the greatest days in my life, because we won 2-1. I scored both the English goals and we'd beaten Scotland at Hampden for the first time in twenty-three years.

I'll never forget the Glasgow papers that night. They put great black lines across the page as though they were in mourning. I remember the goals well, both scored with the feet. It was a hard game and Jack Hill, our centre half, had split his eye open in a collision. He went to outside right and Joe Hulme, the Arsenal winger, took his place in the middle. During the game Joe and I had a chat and I said to him: "Look Joe, I think I can beat those two wingers down the field, so get the ball down the middle and see what happens." So that's just what Joe did and it came off just as we planned.

When the ball came down the middle I hit it from about thirty yards and it flew in.

You could have heard a pin drop at Hampden Park when that happened.

A few minutes later the same thing happened again, but this time I hit the ball with the other foot and it went in the opposite side of the goalkeeper.

When it was all over the F.A. officials, who were all amateurs, came into the dressing room and went round and congratulated the players.

One of them said to me: "Well, I don't know, Dean, that you had such a great game but you got two goals." Well, you can imagine how I felt at that remark seeing as we hadn't beaten Scotland at Glasgow for so long. Fortunately, a lot of other people thought differently about what I had done.

In those days, England didn't play as many internationals as they do nowadays. You could only get caps for playing against Scotland, Wales and Ireland. But after the season was over, England played matches in Belgium, France and Luxembourg and I played in all three. We beat Belgium 9-1 in Brussels and I scored three, beat France 6-0 and I got two and Luxembourg 5-2 and I scored three.

So one way and another 1927 was a great year for me. In those days I was earning £8 a week playing for Everton. When you played for England you didn't get any wages from your club because you were only on contract for them.

We could get £6 for playing for England but on the night before the match they had the audacity to ask us if we wanted the medal or the money. Naturally, most of us went for the medal and that's all we got for playing for our country.

Football was very hard in those days. I would say it was much harder and tougher to play in that it is today, by a long way. You don't see many players today having serious operations or being crippled for life. There were a lot of them in my day.

The season after I broke the scoring record I'll always remember because I had a lot of operations. It was a bad one for me personally. Throughout my career I had fifteen major operations and Harry Cooke seemed to spend his life in hospital with me at that time. I had broken bones, the bones taken out of my ankles, broken ribs, broken toes and cartilage operations.

Harry Cooke put the bones and cartilage in pickle and when new fellows joined the club the first thing Harry did was to show them these bones.

The big difference then was that we played in real boots. From what I can see today they play in carpet slippers.

In those days, if the boot went in you didn't go rolling over on the ground and then get up to take the free kick. You stayed down because you were really injured. You had to wait for the stretcher or be helped off on somebody's shoulder.

There was a lot of very hard men around in those days, especially up Yorkshire way, some really tough ones.

Because players were injured so often, most clubs had a big playing staff. I think the record was forty-two professionals at Everton in one season.

That 28-29 season for me was like an operation year. I'd scored a lot of goals the previous year and a lot of players in a lot of teams were getting their own back.

A lot of them used to say to me: "Wait 'til next year and I'll get you", – and some of them did. I remember that season I had had a bone taken out of my foot. In my first match when I came back, against Huddersfield, I collided with the goalkeeper and put my cartilage out.

I went straight back into the same nursing home I had just left.

The lads were playing hard but the season was nothing like as good as the previous one, and it was clear that eventually we were heading for relegation. You see, when I was out injured, they didn't have another regular centre forward and the team really began to slump. At the end of that season we were near the bottom. The next season we went down into the Second Division.

Dixie challenging in typical
fashion for England

Chapter Eight

We score nine at Goodison and I bag four before half-time

Everton went into the Second Division for season 1929-30 for the first time in the history of the club. Nine months later we were back in the First Division after picking up 61 points, which was then a Second Division record and has only been equalled since, I understand, by Spurs.

Although the previous season had been a bad one for us, we had signed three forwards who were to become great names at Goodison – Tom Johnson, Jimmy Stein and Jimmy Dunn.

But the defence hadn't been too great in the relegation year and before we started in the Second Division we signed Ben Williams, Lachie MacPherson and Bill Bocking. There were one or two others who joined the club as well, but the forward line hadn't changed.

It usually read: Critichley, Dunn, Dean, Johnson and Stein. Sometimes Martin played in place of Johnson. There were a lot of changes from the team which had won the Championship in 1928, two years earlier.

We really set the Second Division on fire that season. We broke records wherever we went.

We started right by going to Plymouth for the first match of the season and beat them 3-2. Later on we went there again in the F.A. Cup and won 2-0 that time. Those were the days. There was a time that season when we scored a tremendous number of goals. We used to hit 7, 8 at home and actually beat Plymouth 9-1 at Goodison on a day when I scored four before half-time. Away we usually won by 3 or 4 goals. Wherever we went it was obvious our opponents were scared of us. You could see that clearly. We knew how well we could play, we knew what we were going to do and we did it.

Our attacking play was based on the same style as we'd used to win the title – two good wingers who could cross the ball to me and I would either nod it in or nod it back to the inside forwards.

Dunn and Johnson scored about 40 goals between them and I got about 39 in the league and nine in the cup myself.

In the Plymouth game when we scored nine, I didn't get any in the second half and people used to say: "Why did you ease up?"

We weren't easing up at all. It was just that the other team were trying a bit harder, but it was really a pantomime. I think we scored 38 goals in 7 or 8 matches at home.

Obviously we won the Second Division by a street. We'd won the promotion race just after Christmas.

We should have won the F.A. Cup that season as well because we had a wonderful run up to the semi-final.

We played West Brom at Old Trafford in the Semi. They had a couple of good players that we used to call the Shaw Brothers, one a fullback and the other a centre half, but they weren't any relation.

The semi-final looked a cake-walk for us. We'd already beaten West Brom twice in the League that season. I'd scored in both those games and it looked a foregone conclusion that we'd get to Wembley that season.

But we missed chance after chance. The goals we missed that day were unbelievable.

Then they scored a goal from near the halfway line and from near the touchline. It was Tommy Glidden who scored it. All he wanted to do was get rid of the ball. He just hit it as hard as he could in the general direction of the goal from way out.

But our goalkeeper, Bill Coggins, had come out of goal. When the ball was in the air he could see he'd made a bloomer in coming out so far, otherwise the ball would have landed in his hands. As it was it dropped over his head and went into the empty net for the winning goal.

That goal was good enough to get West Brom to Wembley and they went on to win the Cup.

I tried the hardest I could to score at Old Trafford. I was knocked around a bit that day and I had two pairs of shorts pulled off me. I remember it well because twice the players had to gather round me while Old Harry brought me out a fresh pair to put on.

But if ever a team should have won we should have done so that day. It was really the only time we went wrong the whole season.

I used to take a lot of battering but I never complained because it was no use. That's how the game was played in those days.

As I said earlier, I suffered about 15 major football injuries in my time, but I never complained and I am proud of the fact that throughout my career I was never spoken to or cautioned by a referee.

In fact, there was only one referee who ever spoke to me during a match. He was Lol Harper of Stourbridge.

He called me over in one match and I thought: "What have I done now?" He just said, "Do you want a mint to suck, Billy?" I said, "Yes, thanks very much."

So Everton went straight back into the First Division and it was the start of our great hat-trick, which stood as a record in League football – Second Division Championship, the League Championship and the F.A. Cup in three successive seasons.

Chapter Nine

I said to my defensive shadow: 'I'm going to the lavatory, are you going to follow?'

Many people think that the Everton team that won the First Division in season 31/32 was one of the greatest teams the club has ever had. As far as I was concerned it was the best Everton team I ever played in and I also think that I was at the peak of my career at about that time.

I was 24 and felt really great having got over all the major injuries.

I had been captain for a few years by then but I was really proud to be skipper of this team. The usual line up was: Sagar, Williams, Creswell, Britton, Gee Thompson, Critchley, Dunn, Dean, Johnson and Stein.

Tommy White played a lot of games as well, either at centre half or at inside forward. Archie Clark also played a lot of games that season.

It was a really tough season and we were chased all the way by Arsenal, who had won the title the previous season, and Sheffield Wednesday. We were at the top for a good part of the time and when you're in that position every team you meet tries to beat you extra hard.

But we had a pretty good team, as I've said.

I remember one particular match against Arsenal that season. I recall it as the start of what has become known as the third-back game. I scored 38 goals that season and Herbert Chapman, the Arsenal manager, was always on about tactics and things so he decided to do something to stop me.

The Arsenal centre half in those days was Herbie Roberts - we were the best of pals, we used to go golfing together.

That day little Jimmy Dunn and Tosh Johnson were the inside forwards and during the game I said: "There's something wrong here, Tosh. This big fellow, Roberts, is walking everywhere with me. I'll take him for a walk so one of you stay down the middle."

This went on for a bout 20 minutes until I turned to Roberts and said: "I'm going off." And I walked to the line. He said, "Where are you going to, Bill?" I said, "What's the idea? What are you following me for?"

He replied: "Mr Chapman told me wherever you go I've got to go with you." I said, "Well come on then, I'm going to the lavatory. Are you going to come with me?"

Of course all the spectators standing by the line heard what we'd said to each other and it brought the place down.

Anyway, Roberts started a new defensive system that day and it's still being played to this day – the third-back game.

I remember another game at Leicester. They had a centre forward called Chandler and he was a real tearaway. I told Teddy Sagar about him and said, "If this man Chandler comes running at you, move out of the way or otherwise you and the ball will finish in the back of the net." You could charge a goalkeeper in those days, providing it was a shoulder charge.

Before long the very thing I'd warned Sagar about happened. Chandler charged in and Sagar was on his bottom with the ball in his hand and both in the net – Leicester were one up.

We got a couple of goals and were leading 2-1 when Chandler came charging through again. Teddy Sagar was very nimble in those days and was ready for him. He dodged out of his way and Chandler ran right through into the net and pulled it down on top of him and finished up, net and all, over the wall at the back of the goal.

As a matter of fact, Chandler was a rival of mine for the England place in those days so I was rather pleased with what had happened.

The memory of Chandler reminds me of another great character – Elisha Scott, the Liverpool goalkeeper who was the greatest I have ever seen.

I remember once we were playing at Anfield and just as I was going into the players' entrance I met Elisha. His first words to me were, "You'll get no goals today you black-headed so-and-so."

I said to him: "If I don't lick you today I'm going right back to work on the railway." I scored three goals against him in the first nine minutes. Elisha's language was unbelievable and the things he called me.

Jimmy Jackson, who was called the Parson, was on of the Liverpool fullbacks that day and he just couldn't stand Elisha's lingo and the words he came out with.

Just after I had scored the third goal, Jimmy turned to me and said, "William, I shall never play in front of this man again."

As a matter of fact, he didn't because the next week Liverpool dropped Elisha and played Arthur Riley in goal.

But Elisha was the greatest I've ever seen. You can have Swift, Trautmann, Banks, Wilson - you can have them all. I'll take Elisha Scott. He only had 21 goals scored against him in two seasons so he couldn't have been too bad could he?

Around that time, about 1930, Liverpool had a good team with players like Lucas, McKinlay, Wadsworth, Bromilow and Forshaw. But the man I remember most in my playing days against Liverpool was Elisha. He and I used to have some great battles. But about this time I'm talking about it was Everton who had the better team.

While we were winning our three successes in three years Liverpool didn't win anything. But our games against them were always great whatever position we were in the League.

As far as I was concerned, I was still the regular England centre forward at that time. I played for England even when Everton were in the Second Division and I think I had about four seasons as the regular England leader. But I still had one great ambition – to win the F.A. Cup.

GREAT SCOT: Elisha was a world class keeper, but he swore like a trooper

Chapter Ten

Veteran Warney Cresswell was in our Wembley dressing room smoking his pipe.
I lit up a cigarette and said:
Let City wait!

By the start of season 32/33 the Everton team was in really tremendous form.

I used to think it was like an orchestra. Everybody was in tune with everyone else's play.

We didn't need to practice moves, we all knew what each other was going to do. Lads like Jimmy Dunn and Tosh Johnson could read the game and they knew exactly where I was going to put the ball to them when it came to me in the air. Everything was instinctive. Most of us had played together for three or four years and when we beat teams like Chelsea by eight or Sheffield Wednesday by nine you didn't need to practice moves. The moves were all there all the time.

At the start of the season I very much wanted to win the Cup because we'd won the League Championship the season before.

The way we were playing we didn't have to try any harder, just play our usual game because we knew it was paying off.

We beat Leicester 3-2 in the first round and when we came into the dressing room afterwards I said to the lads, "Well done. Don't alter what you're doing, just keep to the same tune."

The only time throughout the Cup run when we might have come unstuck was in the semi-final at Wolverhampton against West Ham. Things didn't come off for us that day and Dick Watson, the West Ham centre forward, could have beaten us. He tried to draw Ted Sagar out of his goal and put the ball past him. If he had shot first time he would have scored but as Ted came out he slipped but still managed to grab hold of the ball.

The semi-final was by far the most difficult game we played that season because we won all our other matches pretty well.

In fact, the final against Manchester City at Wembley was so easy. The bookies were backing 7-4 on City and I thought it was a ridiculous price. I liked a bet myself and I thought I'd have a go that time, but I didn't.

When we got to Wembley we went out to look at the pitch but we had been to see it a couple of days previously.

Just before the game started a commissionaire came to our dressing room door and said, "Get ready to come out. Manchester City are just going down the tunnel."

I said, "It's all right. Don't worry, we'll catch them up later. Shut the door."

All the lads said to me, "Come on, Bill, we'll have to hurry up."

But old Warney Creswell was sitting there as calm as ever, smoking his pipe. So to keep him company I lit a cigarette and I said to the lads, "There's plenty of time. Let them wait." So they did wait in the tunnel so that we could line up with them. They must have waited a good few minutes for us. When I got alongside Sam Cowan, the City captain, he was holding a football in his hand and you could see how nervous he was. I said to him, "That ball is shaking in your hand." So I got hold of his hand and said, "Put your other hand on top and stop the ball from shaking." You should have seen him.

It wasn't long before Jimmy Stein scored the first goal. The ball had been pushed down the middle and I nodded it back to Tosh Johnson who placed a great pass between the fullback and the halfback for Jimmy Stein.

Jimmy was very fast in those days. He ran through them and round them and didn't hesitate. He hit the ball on the run. It never left the ground and it went right in the far corner of the net.

After that there was only one team in it. You didn't have to tell Cliff Britton or Tosh Johnson what to do and early in the second half Cliff got this ball just in the right position on the halfway line. I knew exactly what he was going to do and he put it right over into the goalmouth.

I went up with Landford, the City goalkeeper. He could see me coming in and he took his eye off the ball. All I had to do was go up and nod it in, just a flick of the head and that was the second.

I've read since that some people think I didn't score that goal – that the ball went in directly from Cliff's centre or that Langford pushed it in himself. But I can tell you that I did head the ball and score.

The third goal came soon afterwards. Albert Geldard took a corner on the right. Before he did I said to Jimmy Dunn, "Stand near the corner of the penalty area."

This was what he intended to do but Albert hit the corner very hard and it came straight to Dunn instead of me.

Jimmy Dunn headed it right back across the goalmouth and as Langford hesitated, looking at me and thinking I was going to move in to head the ball again, Jimmy's header went straight past him into the far corner of the net.

Jimmy Dunn ran like mad all round Wembley. He went so far I thought he was the hare on the greyhound track.

So that was our 3-0 Wembley win – one of the easiest games we'd had all season.

The one man on the City side I felt sorry for particularly was their inside-left Jimmy McMullan because it was his last game in football and the last chance, of course, that he'd ever have of getting a Cup medal.

I'll never forget going up to the Royal Box to receive the Cup from the Duchess of York, who later became Queen. She congratulated me and said it was a very good game and that she had enjoyed it.

So that was Wembley 1933 and I had then won every honour. The Cup winner's medal completed the collection.

Chapter Eleven

I nearly lost the lid of the FA Cup under a train

On the Saturday night after we had won the F.A. Cup by beating Manchester City at Wembley, we all went to a big reception at a London West End hotel.

Lord Derby was in the chair and after the dinner was over I went up to him and said to him, "I believe you've got a good horse in the Chester Vase this year."

He said, "Yes. My trainer tells me that if it wins the Chester Vase it will win the Derby."

The name of the horse was Hyperion so I told all the lads what Lord Derby had said and we all had a good bet on it for the Derby. On the day of the race we were in Copenhagen on tour. We were all sitting in a beer garden in the Hotel Cosmopolitan having a few beers. We were listening to the radio and suddenly we heard this announcement in English, "Here is the result of the English Derby – first Hyperion." At that we all jumped to our feet, knocked over the table and in our excitement spilt all the beer on it. Some of it splashed over a gentleman sitting at the next table.

I went to him to apologise and he said, "It's all right. I've enjoyed every moment of your conversation."

I looked at him closely and saw that it was that famous old film star, Jean Hersholt. I offered to pay for his suit to be cleaned but he said, "Don't bother. I'd like all you lads to have a drink with me. It's been very nice listening to you all."

But to go back to the days immediately after the Cup Final, we stayed overnight in London on the Sunday night and came back to Liverpool by train on the Monday.

On the train the Chairman, old Bill Cuff, said to me, "Billy, take the Cup right through the train. It's a special train with lots of our supporters on it so let them have a look at it."

So I started off down the train with the Cup with a few of the lads. Well, of course, by the time I'd got halfway down the train we'd had a few drinks with the people and were all feeling great.

When the train was pulling out of Crewe for home there were hundreds of people standing in the fields and lining the track. They had come miles to see the Cup so I opened the window and showed it to them. As I showed it through the open window the lid fell off. As it happened, Tommy Johnson was standing close to me and he just caught the lid before it dropped on the railway line.

We got a fantastic reception at Lime Street when we arrived. We went from the station to the Town Hall in a horse-drawn wagonette, sitting in the open on the top so that everyone could see the Cup and the players. I'll never forget the people cheering as we went along Lime Street and Dale Street.

After the reception at the Town Hall we went by coach to Goodison Park. The ground had been opened to the public and the place was packed. We went out onto the pitch and walked round to show them the Cup.

We had one more match to play in the League against Sheffield Wednesday and that ended a great season - the end of our hat-trick sequence.

ABOVE: Dean proudly showing off the FA Cup after Everton's triumph in 1933

ABOVE: A typically strong challenge from Dean against Spurs in an FA Cup fifth round replay at White Hart Lane on February 22nd, 1937. He scored twice but Everton lost 4-3.

LEFT: Dixie at Goodison, just a year before his record-breaking 60 goals.

ALWAYS HAD A GOOD ENGINE: Dixie knew how to find top gear!

ABOVE: Dixie fires home in typical fashion, leaving the opposing goal-keeper with no chance.

LEFT: Dixie pictured with his friend Ellis Rimmer. The pair were team-mates for Birkenhead Schoolboys and Tranmere.

RIGHT: In derby action, Dixie holds off Liverpool's William Steel in September 1934. He scored the only goal in the Blues' win at Goodison.

ABOVE: Dixie's aerial ability was second to none as Huddersfield Town found to their cost in September 1927.

ABOVE: Dixie shares a joke with Everton team-mate Tom Griffiths.

RIGHT: Fully focused as always as he prepares to lead the Everton attack.

LEFT: Looking dapper as he poses proudly during his Goodison heyday.

BELOW: Dixie with, from left, team-mates George Martin, Tommy White, Billy Coggins and Tom Griffiths.

ABOVE: Dixie pictured in the second row of the 1929-30 squad photograph.

*BELOW: One of Dixie's top strike partners, Tommy White,
scores in a 4-2 win over Sunderland in January 1932.*

ABOVE: Aston Villa's goalkeeper feels the force of a typically robust Dixie challenge.

BELOW: The Duchess of York presents Dixie with the FA Cup following the Blues' 3-0 defeat of Manchester City at Wembley in 1933. The Duchess went on to become Queen but Dixie was football's King of the day.

ABOVE: An Everton group photo with the League Championship trophy after Dixie had completed his feat of 60 league goals in the final match of the 1927-28 season. From left to right are: Harry Cooke (trainer), Ted Critchley, George Martin, Jerry Kelly, Warney Cresswell (captain), John O'Donnell, Will Cuff (chairman), Hunter Hart, Dixie, Arthur Davies, Tony Weldon, Ted Virr and Alec Troup.

RIGHT: Welcoming winger
Torry Gillick to Goodison in
December 1935.
The £8,000 buy from Glasgow
Rangers would be a provider
of many goals for Dixie.

RIGHT: As this picture shows, Dixie gave everything for Everton and was always prepared to sweat it out in the cause.

LEFT: Away from football, Dixie enjoyed pitching in with the local baseball team Liverpool Caledonians.

ABOVE: Demonstrating the power of his heading in scoring one of his four goals in the 9-1 FA Cup defeat of Southport in February 1931.

BELOW: Everton's 1963 League title winning skipper Roy Vernon with Dixie - another man who captained the Blues to the championship.

RIGHT: Everton's goalscoring angel shows off his heading technique during that 9-1 FA Cup thrashing of Southport in 1931. The heavily touched up image almost looks like a painting.

ABOVE: Dixie pounces to net the historic header against Arsenal which gave him 60 league goals for the 1927/28 season.

ABOVE: Evertonians saw 12 goals at Goodison on the afternoon of October 17th 1931. Inspired by four players who all won England caps, the Blues were in great form. Pictured, from left to right, are: Ted Sagar, Tommy White, Tommy Johnson and Dixie.

*RIGHT: Dixie adds to his awesome goal
tally with another trademark header.*

*ABOVE: Three of the greatest Everton forwards of all
time: Tommy Lawton, Alex Young and Dixie.*

Dixie holds the FA Cup on his shoulder in 1933 flanked by delighted team-mates.

ABOVE: Everton's Seventies striking star Bob Latchford takes a few tips from the master on board when Dixie dropped in at Bellefield to pass on some handy hints.

RIGHT: With three lions on his shirt, Dixie was as prolific as always. He was capped by his country 16 times, scoring 18 goals.

RIGHT: Dixie, number nine, pictured in action in the 1933 FA Cup final. He is seen looking on as the third goal hits the back of the net in the 3-0 defeat of Manchester City at Wembley.

ABOVE: Always modest. Dixie (at the back) and his Everton team-mates take some time out during a training session.

RIGHT: The Everton team of 1931-32 scored well over 100 goals on their way to the League Championship. The team is, back row, from left: Jock Thomson, Archie Clark, Charlie Gee, Ted Sagar, Ben Williams, Warney Cresswell, Bill Bocking, Harry Cooke (trainer). Front: Ted Critchley, Jimmy Dunn, Dixie, Tommy Johnson, Jimmy Stein and Tommy White.

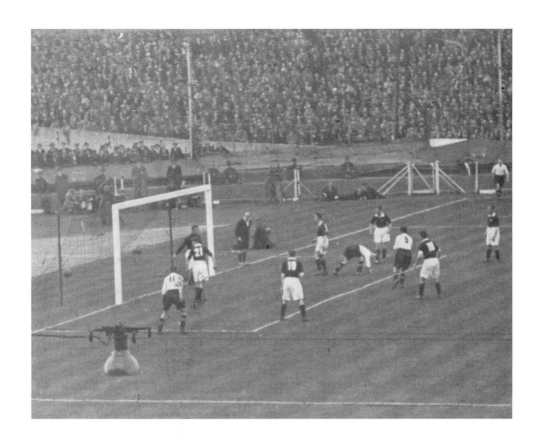

Dixie with another footballing legend, Matt Busby, either side of the Lord Mayor, Alderman JJ Cleary.

ABOVE: Dixie shares a moment with Joe Mercer.

RIGHT: Dixie shows his daughter Barbara the statuette which marked his inclusion into the football Hall of Fame.

*BELOW: Captains together - Dixie Dean with captain W.B. Coyle
of the Canadian Pacific liner the Duchess of York.*

BELOW: A Spanish defender clears the ball off Dixie's toe during an international at Highbury in 1931. Dixie scored his final international goal in England's 7-1 win.

ABOVE: Another day, another goal. Dixie leaves another goalkeeper beaten.

RIGHT: Outside the doorway of his Chester pub, The Dublin Packet.

LEFT: Dixie was never happier than when he was in the blue and white of Everton.

ABOVE: Heads I win! Dixie powers home a header against Bolton in a 3-0 win at Goodison on December 29, 1928. He hit a hat-trick in Everton's 3-0 win.

BELOW: A keen spectator after he had hung up his boots, Dixie followed every minute of this Territorial Army Cup tie in March 1949.

LEFT: A young Dixie takes centre-stage in a team line-up.

BELOW: Dixie shares some memories with his old team-mate Joe Mercer at a dinner held in their honour by Tranmere Rovers.

....

BELOW: Dixie watches as a Sheffield United defender concedes a corner during a
2-0 defeat of the Blades at Goodison Park in March 1927.

ABOVE: The original third back, Arsenal's Herbert Roberts, shadows Dixie as Gunners manager Herbert Chapman brought in a new defensive strategy in an attempt to stop the Blues' great number nine.

LEFT: On and off the pitch, Dixie always had a smile on his face.

RIGHT: Dixie was always ready to talk football.

*BELOW: Dixie shaking hands with John Moores at a
League Championship dinner in 1963.*

*RIGHT: Dixie with the haul of medals he
won in his astonishing career.*

RIGHT: Peter Gray, assistant caretaker of regional history at the Merseyside Maritime Museum, with a pair of 1930s football boots and medals which made up part of the Dixie Dean Exhibition held in 1992.

Liverpool goalkeeper Kane and full-back Tennant look on as Dixie shows off his exquisite control during a derby at Anfield in 1935.

ABOVE: Famous Liverpool Echo cartoonist George Green hailed Everton's 1927-28 champions with this tribute.

BELOW: Dixie has a go on the other side of the camera at an Everton photocall!

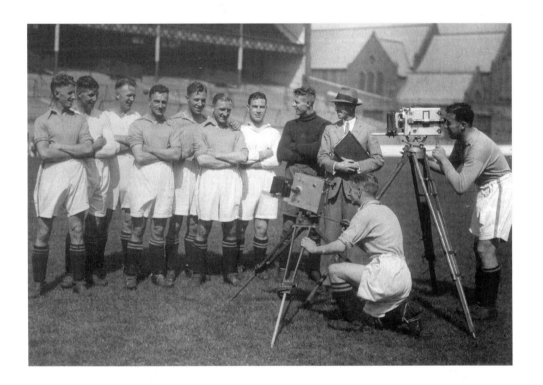

Chapter Twelve

Row with Dresden captain over ball size. No problem, I kicked his size 4 over the stand roof!

We went off on tour to Denmark. We used to tour quite a lot during the summer with Everton in my day.

We went to Denmark twice and Germany and also to the Canary Isles one year. I remember once when we were playing Dresden in Germany. The previous year it had taken England all their time to beat the full German team in an international and I had taken with me the programme from that match.

The night before Everton's game with Dresden the famous coach, Jimmy Hogan, who was working in Germany at that time, came to me and said, "You've got nothing to worry about tomorrow. You're only playing a club team."

But I produced the international programme and checked it with the Dresden team that was going to play us the next day and they had ten internationals in the side – ten of the men who had played against England the previous year. They were trying a right fiddle against us.

Their best player was an inside forward called Hoffman. I'd played against him in the England team and knew what a great player he was.

Before the match I said to Bill Bocking, who was going to mark him, "You'll be seeing a lot of this Hoffman if you don't give him the old shoulder charge nice and hard."

Before long Hoffman scored a goal and I shouted down to our defence, "Don't forget the next time." So the next time Hoffman moved down on goal he was sorted out and they took him off on a stretcher. We went on to beat them in the end.

There was a funny incident before the start of the match. We had taken a supply of size 5 footballs with us and the Dresden team had agreed to use it. When I went to the middle to toss up with the Jerry captain, he was carrying a size 4 ball that he wanted to use. It was just a kid's ball and we didn't want to use it.

I said to him, "This is the ball we're going to use", and put the size 5 down on the centre spot. The Jerry captain kicked it away and put his ball down so I kicked that away.

The referee was trying to stop all this when I said to the Jerry captain, "All right, give me your ball."

I carried it over to the touchline and the captain and the referee followed me. When I got to the line I kicked the size 4 ball right over the stand and out of the ground. I turned to the referee and said, "Now, we'll play with this one - the size 5 ball."

We did and won. But we didn't have a very happy tour that year and in the last match in Nuremberg Jimmy Stein broke a leg.

Chapter Thirteen

Am I the only England player to be sin-binned in an international?

In the Thirties England didn't play many foreign teams, except when they went on summer tours. But I remember one famous match against Spain at Highbury because it had been built up beforehand as though the Spaniards were going to give us a real test.

The big personality in the Spanish team was the goalkeeper, Zamora. He was regarded as the best in the world at the time and he used to get £40 per week while the England lads were only on £8.

But he didn't look so great that day. We beat them 7-1 and we were three up in about ten minutes.

I remember one particular goal by Eric Brook, the Manchester City winger. He had a terrific shot and in this incident Jackie Smith crossed the ball and I nodded it back to Brook. I could see he was shaping to hit it straight back so I fell down out of the way and Brook gave this ball a terrific crack and it flew just across the top of my head into the back of the net. Sammy Crooks of Derby was on the other wing and I nodded a few goals from his centres. Towards the end of the match the Spaniards were so worried about this move that they thought I was going to score every time Sammy crossed the ball. The Spanish defence followed me so that Sammy was able to bring the ball in himself and score easily.

There was another funny incident in an England match in Paris. Sammy Weaver, the Newcastle wing half, was in the England team that day and he was famous for his long throw-in.

When Sammy got a throw-in the England forwards ran towards him taking the Spanish defenders with them because they knew what Sammy was going to do. There was only the goalkeeper and myself left near the goal and when Sammy threw the ball over the heads of everybody, I had an easy job to nod it into the net. The French spectators went mad with that particular goal.

There was another time when I was sent off in an international playing against Belgium in Antwerp.

Tommy Whitaker, the Arsenal trainer, was in charge of the England team that day and he ran onto the pitch and said "You've been sent off for ten minutes."

I said, "What are you talking about?" There had been an incident a few minutes before when the Belgium goalkeeper had caught the ball as I was standing shoulder to shoulder with him. I didn't charge him but our shoulders were just touching and he fell in the net with the ball.

I thought it was a good goal but the referee sent me off for ten minutes.

TWO LEGENDS: Dean and Spanish goalkeeper Zamora

Chapter Fourteen

Tommy Lawton was signed to replace me, but I was the first to meet him at Lime Street Station and show him the ropes

For most of the years I was at Everton Tom McIntosh was the manager but he was more like a secretary than a manager today. Harry Cooke, the trainer, was in complete charge of the players, being responsible for training and everything to do with them.

After we had won the Cup in '33 we had a couple of very ordinary seasons at Everton and I realised that I was slowing up and could not do what I used to be able to do. So around 1936 Everton bought Tommy Lawton from Burnley for £6,000.

I realised he had been bought to take my place and I accepted that. In fact, I went down to the station to meet the kid when he came to Liverpool for the first time.

He was only 17 and he was rather like I had been when I first joined Everton. He was about an inch taller than me but he had a marvellous physique – a lovely built lad.

I helped him a lot in his early days at Everton. I used to take him out in the afternoons on the little practice ground at Goodison. We had a tennis net strung up and headed the ball backward and forwards to each other across the net.

I did this myself to help Tommy. I wasn't told to. He was a good header of the ball when he came to Everton but I like to think that I helped him a lot and brought him up.

When he first came to Goodison he played inside right to me and I remember one famous match when we played together. It was in a Cup replay at Tottenham and later Arthur Rowe, who played for Spurs in that game, said to me: "We were licked. We were well beaten."

With only a few minutes to go we were leading 3-1. I moved down the middle with the ball, was brought down and it was a clear penalty. The referee allowed it and I was just about to take this penalty when the Spurs players rushed over to the referee and told him that one of the linesmen was flagging.

The linesman said that the ball had gone out of play before I had got it so the referee gave a throw-in to Spurs instead of a penalty to us.

From that throw-in they scored to make it 3-2 and they got two more in the last three minutes to beat us 4-3.

But I remember Tommy had scored the first goal that day. It was a really great effort.

The last two centre forwards I knew in my time were Tommy Lawton and Hughie Gallagher. If I had to buy anybody as a manager and had the money it would be those two at their best. They were very different types of players. Lawton played the game like I did - good in the air and always eager to have a shot for goal. But Gallagher was a different type of player altogether.

He was small and very clever with the ball. He could beat two or three men in a short distance. He was brilliant with the ball.

He was a good little sport as well. He took some kicks in his time because he used to aggravate his opponents with his cleverness.

Chapter Fifteen

The last Goodison milestone
– I break Bloomer's record

I know that a lot of people these days say that the players of my era used to drink too much, didn't train very hard and that we had a far too easy life compared to the top players of today. My answer is, in one word: "Ridiculous."

I'm not saying that the players didn't have a few beers, but it was always after a match. The first people who asked me to have a drink after the game would be the directors and we only used to drink beer. I have never drunk spirits or wines in my life, even to this day.

We used to be able to have a few drinks on a Saturday night, Sunday and Monday and then we'd pack it in for the rest of the week. We trained hard for the rest of the week. We made ourselves really fit and nobody was going to be daft enough to undo all that training by going on the beer the night before the match.

Training on Tuesday morning was really tough – physically tough – any beer that we had drunk over the weekend soon came out of us in those days. Then we'd look after ourselves for the rest of the week.

I was never affected by the Everton fans on remarks when I was at my peak. I used to stop and chat with them in the street. They were all anxious to know what was happening and their praise never made me big-headed.

It's lovely to know that people still remember you. I always enjoyed taking my different trophies around to Youth Clubs to show them off to the kids.

I always signed autographs, day in and day out and I'll never forget the Everton fans for the way they treated me, not only when playing, but even after I had finished with the club.

I felt that these fans belonged to me and I belonged to them. I was born and bred an Evertonian and I always will be one. I would have liked to have finished my playing days at Everton, but it was not to be.

But before I left Everton there was one other milestone I passed in my career at Goodison and that was when I broke Steve Bloomer's scoring record in 1936.

Bloomer's record was 352 League goals for Derby County and I broke that record in a match against Sheffield Wednesday.

I remember it well. The ball came across from a corner, taken by Jackie Coulter. Five Sheffield players were standing on the goal line between the goalposts. So instead of heading it up or trying to place it in one of the corners, I got up and headed the ball down to allow it to bounce over the line. I thought the ball would get past their legs quickly then it would go by their heads or the goalkeepers hands.

That's how I scored that particular goal and the first man to congratulate me was my old Birkenhead pal, Ellis Rimmer, who was playing for the Wednesday that day.

I have often been asked what was the secret of my ability to head the ball. I must say it was instinct, a gift born in me, but as I was going up for the centre I knew exactly where I wanted to place the ball with the header. I knew which side of the goalkeeper I wanted to place it.

I used to try to give the ball just a slight flick with the forehead because in that way you can place the ball wide of the goalkeeper.

I knew where the goalkeeper was standing, and I always thought a flick was more effective. If I had made a half turn in the air and headed it square with my forehead I couldn't have got the same pace with the ball as I did.

Of course, a great deal depended on the men who were marking the centre. I was lucky at Everton with people like Alec Troup, Jimmy Stein, Albert Geldard, Cliff Britton and Jackie Coulter. They used to hit the ball over hard and fast and it was easy for me to make those flick headers and get real pace on the ball.

Even today I get letters from Everton fans asking me about famous matches and famous goals. Some of them seem to remember every move I made on the pitch.

I left Everton in the 1937/8 season. Tommy Lawton was well established by then in the first team and I had been playing quite a bit in the reserves.

In fact, while I was in the side we won the Central League Championship, so that was another medal to add to the collection. I never thought I'd get that one, but I did.

I would have liked to have stayed to the end at Everton but the break came in 1938 when I was transferred to Notts. County. I never thought of going into football management. I always believe that managers and chairman and directors are people who can't sleep at night with all the worry they have. I like to have a good night's sleep so I didn't fancy management or even trying to do a bit of coaching.

When I left Everton I was strong and thought I'd be able to find another job somewhere easily but I knew that when my playing career was over I wanted to get out of football completely.

I would still follow the game, of course, but I didn't want any official part in it at all.

Chapter Sixteen

Charged with being brought home drunk from Blackpool on the back of a lorry when I was actually having dinner with my chairman!

The first time I knew that my relationship with Everton had changed came on a night at the Exchange Hotel that I will never forget.

I have to say that things had not been easy for me for some time before that because I just couldn't get on with Theo Kelly who had been the club secretary.

That night I had gone to the Exchange Hotel to attend the Liverpool Bookies dinner and I was all decked out in my evening suit.

But the Everton directors were in a room at the hotel and I was called in to see them. They were all there headed by the chairman, old Will Cuff. He said to me, "Now, William, about this affair a week last Wednesday night. We've been told that you were brought from Blackpool on the back of a lorry and you were rotten drunk."

I denied it immediately. I said to Mr. Cuff, "This is supposed to have happened a week last Wednesday, is that right?" He said, "How should I know?"

I said, "You should know because you should remember who I had dinner with that particular night."

He thought for a while but said nothing and then I said, "Who did I have coffee with at midnight?"

Then it dawned on him. He smashed his fist onto the table, looked across at the other directors and Kelly and said, "Bill Dean was in my home that particular night. He had opened a Youth Club for us at Gateacre and he had a meal and coffee with Mrs. Cuff and myself at our home. So he couldn't have been coming back from Blackpool that night."

That stopped that little incident but I could sense from this that all sorts of lies were being told about me and there were some queer things going on at the time.

So what with Tommy Lawton being there – I was glad they had got him – I could see that things had reached breaking point between me and Kelly.

Sometime earlier Sir Lindsay Parkinson, who was the chairman of Blackpool, had asked me to join that club. I met the Blackpool directors and they made me a good offer. I went to see old Cuff and told him about the Blackpool offer and asked him what he thought about it.

He said: "You are not going to leave Everton. You've got a job here for life." So I went straight back to the Adelphi and told the Blackpool directors that I wasn't going to join them.

But after that incident at the Exchange Hotel, things went from bad to worse until one day I got a phone call to go to Goodison. When I arrived there were some directors from Notts County there and I was told that they wanted to sign me.

I was really fed up with the Everton set up at that time so I agreed to sign for County and I joined them in March 1938 – 13 years almost to the day after I had signed for Everton from Tranmere Rovers.

Notts County paid Everton £3,000 for me – the same fee that Everton had paid Tranmere, so after those 13 years at Goodison I suppose you could say it wasn't a bad buy.

I only played a few times for County because it was in the second match that I broke a bone in my foot.

I was in the Nottingham General Hospital for about two months and had to have an operation to remove this bone. When I came out of hospital I was only hobbling about and only managed to play another seven games for Notts County altogether.

While I was at Nottingham I got a letter from the Irish club, Sligo, asking me if I could find them a centre half. I asked one or two players and the first thing they said was, "Isn't it a bit dangerous out there with all this IRA lark going on?" This was in the 1938/39 season and I suppose the IRA was pretty active at that time.

So I couldn't find anybody who wanted to go to Ireland and I told them so. Eventually they cabled me to ask if I would play for them. By then I had got over my foot operation and I was doing a bit of training. Notts County were prepared to let me go so I cabled back to Sligo and arranged to meet their officials in Dublin to discuss terms.

We met in Dublin and we set off right away by train for Sligo. They told me there was a big reception waiting for me there and when the train was about a mile from Sligo I head five explosions. I looked across at the Sligo official and said, "These IRA blokes aren't very good shots are they? They've missed five times." But the Sligo chairman said, "Don't worry, Bill, they were only fog signals exploding on the railway line."

I had a tremendous reception at Sligo and in my short time with them I had some of my greatest days in football.

This was in the 1938/39 season. The club owed a Mrs. Reed £200 for the rent but I managed to keep them going. I started doing one or two of the old tricks, getting four or five goals each match, and the crowds rolled up and I was really glad to be able to help them because they were such nice people. You've heard of the phrase, "They played that game without the ball" and that was rather true of Irish football at that time.

I remember playing in an Irish Cup tie against Dundoran. Five players were sent off, three for Dundoran and two from Sligo and before the end the referee was carried off too.

It was quite a carry-on there week after week but we didn't have a bad season. We finished second to Shamrock Rovers in the League and only lost 1-0 after two replays to Shelbourne in the final of the Irish Cup.

We had a banquet after that match and I had to tell them that I was leaving them. The war had started in England and I had received my call-up papers for the Army.

The Sligo chairman, Charlie Slattery, thanked me for what I'd done during the season, told me that he'd been able to pay Mrs. Reed the £200 they owed her and they had also finished £800 in profit, which was a terrific lot of money for a club like Sligo in those days.

He also gave me a sealed envelope. I thought he'd put a couple of the club's ties in it so I didn't open it until I got on the boat. When I did I found in it 80 brand new pound notes – English notes not Irish. That was a terrific amount from a little club like Sligo and I was very grateful.

Chapter Seventeen

Transferred – by the Army – for defending an Irish mate against a policeman

The last game of football played as a professional was for Irish club Sligo Rovers in December 1940. The same night I was on the boat back to Liverpool to join the army.

When I got home my wife said to me, "You've had another invitation. I've put the letter on the mantle piece."

I said, "Where are we going?" She replied, "It's for you, not us."

It turned out that the invitation was from the King – my calling-up papers. I had to report to a barracks at Formby and in my draft there were a lot of other footballers and boxers whom I knew.

When I was at Formby they asked me to look after the sports arrangements – running the football team and one thing and another. The depot team once played a team of Lancashire internationals on our depot ground. As it happened, Tommy Lawton was in the other team but we had a good side and we beat them about 7-1. There were one or two lads from Scotland Road in our side who could go a bit in football.

From Formby I volunteered to join the tank corps. I thought that I'd had so much trouble with my legs during my football career with so many injuries, that if I was going to cop for it I might as well ride to it as walk.

I was sent to a tank depot at Warminster. I was able to drive because I'd owned a car for some years and eventually I was made a corporal instructor on tanks and Bren gun carriers.

I enjoyed myself at Warminster until one incident changed my army career. The sergeant major, an Irishman, was going on leave and he had to change into civilian clothes because he was travelling to Ireland.

We were having a few drinks together in a pub in Warminster when Paddy got involved in some trouble with a policeman. I stepped in to help, the policeman pushed me and I pushed him back a bit harder. I thought no more about it that night.

But the next day I was hauled up before the colonel who told me that I was in some real trouble because the policeman was in hospital. It seems I had pushed him a bit too hard.

The colonel told me I could either take his punishment or have court marshal. I took his punishment, which was a transfer from Warminster.

I went from there to the 27th Lancers at Pickering, Yorkshire. I was still with the tanks and my unit travelled all over Britain. We were more or less a defence lot in case of an invasion. The unit never went abroad and I stayed with the Lancers until I was demobbed in 1945.

The only football I played during the war years was for the regimental teams. I never guested for any of the big clubs like many footballers did.

When I was demobbed I came back to Merseyside. During the war my home in New Ferry had been blitzed and my wife and three children were living with a couple in Chester.

My wife decided we had to get out of that, get into some business and start to make our own lives again.

I did have a business of my own before the war. I opened a sports outfitting shop in Birkenhead and used the money I had got at Everton – £1,850 in all – to start the business off.

I had a manager in charge and it was going quite well until the war started and that flattened the business. It blew the lot.

Now I had to find myself a new job. There was nothing left for me in football.

I had an old friend who was an official of Chester Northgate Breweries and I asked him if there was a public house of theirs I could have. They offered me the Dublin Packet, which was in the main square of Chester near theTown Hall.

So I took it and I enjoyed my years as a licensee. I was there nearly 15 years altogether but eventually the work became too much for me.

But it was a pretty good life and the brewery was very good to me. I used to have all my trophies and international caps on show behind the bar. There were always blokes coming into the pub, a lot of them Americans from Sealand Aerodrome, asking if they could take a photograph of me with the trophies in the background. It was always packed and I think there were fellows from all over the world who came into the pub to see me.

Chapter Eighteen

Bonanza £9,000 testimonial and I'm comfortable

I'd be about 53 years old when I gave up the licensing business in Chester and started to look round for another job. I wasn't feeling exactly on top of the world when I left the Dublin Packet because I'd only managed to save a couple of hundred quid.

One day, however, I met Dick Searle who was then the chairman of Everton. I told him I was looking for a job – I'd have taken anything – and he said he would ask Mr. John Moores, who was then a director of the club.

I went to see Mr. Moores in his office and he was good enough to find me a job with Littlewoods.

It was Dick Searle who first mentioned arranging a testimonial match for me at Everton and Mr. Moores agreed as well. It was a wonderful thing and I was very grateful. They asked me what teams I would like to play in the testimonial match. I didn't want any players outside Liverpool in the game so I thought it would be a good idea to arrange an international match, England v Scotland, choosing the teams from those then at Liverpool and Everton.

I'd gone through the names of the local players and found that I could get 11 England and 11 Scots for the two teams. I suggested this to Mr. Moores and he agreed right away.

It was a great game at Goodison and there was a crowd of about 40,000. I lead the teams out to the centre and I can't tell you how I felt when I walked onto my old ground again.

I got the receipt from that match, about £9,000, and Mr. Moores kept it for me and invested it all so that I would get the income from it while it continued to build up.

Of course, I continued to follow the game. I've read a lot about the modern-day players on their special training, special meals and special training grounds like Everton have at Bellefield.

We used to train at Bellefield in my day but obviously not to the same extent as they do today.

I would say that club discipline in the game today is tighter than it was when I was playing. We were much more on trust in the old days.

To me, football today seems too regimental. There aren't the characters around in the game as there used to be in my day – men like Jack Tinn of Portsmouth who always wore white spats, or Johnny Cochrane of Sunderland or our own old Tom McIntosh.

He was a good outspoken man, old Tom. He came to me and said, "Now listen, Billy, you've got to win this League. It means a lot to me because it'll put another fiver a week on my wages and you boys have no need to worry, you'll be looked after."

We won two cups for him and put plenty onto his wages but I'll say this for him, he bought the lads a little bit of something.

But even in my day we used to go away for special training. Everton always went to Buxton and when we were having a good run in the cup we'd go there for weeks at a time. I used to be a bit of a practical joker in those days, trying to get the lads in the right frame of mind and cracking a few jokes.

I remember we were at Buxton once and we'd all been given a new pair of flannel trousers from a local firm. We were photographed wearing them as an advertisement.

One Sunday morning, we'd been doing a bit of training on some roadwork and when we got back to the hotel Tosh Johnson was leaning over the bath talking to somebody in it.

I lifted him up and placed him right in, new trousers and all. As he was lying in the bath he laughed his head off so I said, "What's up with you?" He said, "It's all right, I'm wearing your trousers." That was the way we used to carry on, always kidding each other.

Whenever a new player came to the club I went out of my way to make him feel at home. In those days we didn't have youth apprentices and bring them up from kids like they do today. If they wanted somebody they went out and bought him so there were always new faces about each season.

I loved to see those boys come in because I was an Evertonian through and through and if I could help them I would because I wanted them to carry on helping the club when I had finished playing.

Chapter Nineteen

Everton in the 1930s played like an orchestra

The Everton team that won the 1969/70 Championship wouldn't have had a chance with the Everton side in the early 30s when we won that great treble. In those days we played a neater game of football and the players knew each other absolutely. We played like an orchestra.

Nobody was told, "Don't do this" or "Don't do that." We went out there and we knew exactly what we were going to do.

The great difference between the game then and now was in the use of wingers. In my days at Everton we had wingers like Teddy Critchley, Sammy Chedgzoy, Albert Geldard, Alec Troup, Jimmy Stein and Jackie Coulter.

Their job was to go quickly down the wings and centre it hard. It was my job to meet these centres and either have a go at putting it in the net if I thought I was the right distance away, or nod it back to the inside forwards.

You don't see it happening today. When the ball goes out to the wing all the players seem to drop back. It's pushed back to the right half, then it goes to the centre half and he pushes it to somebody else and there's all this up and down, up and down, across, across.

We played direct football – and that is what I mean by good football. People go to see goals and they're not seeing them today.

In those three seasons the Everton players got a tremendous reception wherever we played because we were showing the fans good, direct football and scoring heaps of goals.

We used to be banging in 6, 7 and 8 at a time. It's never been known at any other club.

Before a match we never used to sit down and discuss the players in the team we were going to play. We never said, "We're playing Arsenal this afternoon, so keep an eye on so-and-so because he can do so-and-so."

We never discussed the other side because there was no need to do so. We played our own game and let them do the worrying.

I don't agree that today's game is played any faster than it was in my time. Nowadays we never see wingers as fast and as good as the men I've mentioned. Nowadays there's too much stopping the ball with players dropping back too much.

In my day the players enjoyed it, the spectators enjoyed it and the whole game had much more character and was full of personalities.

I think a lot of the enjoyment has gone out of the modern game. Some of the things that go on make me want to weep.

Take a world famous fellow like Pele. I saw him in a match on television in the World Cup when he went rolling all over the ground, moaning and groaning when he'd been tackled. Then he got up, took the free kick, and scored. He's a good actor that fellow.

But I will say this about the Brazil team in the 1970 World Cup. They were the only side, except perhaps West Germany, who played with genuine wingers who played a wing game as I understand it.

In that World Cup these two Brazilian wingers were really good players – they went down the wings like lightening.

I'm convinced that if English football went back to using the old style wingers we would see a lot more active play and in addition a lot more goals as well.

Mind you, there doesn't seem to be the centre forwards around today as in my time when our main job was to cash in on the work of the wingers.

I felt Joe Royle was one of those modern centre-forwards whose style I could understand.

In my time there were players as good or better than those all over the country – Tommy Lawton, Chandler (Leicester), Harper (Blackburn), Watson (West Ham), George Brown (Villa), J.R. Smith (Bolton) and George Camsell (Middlesbrough). All these chaps had won international caps.

I was on a television programme a couple of years ago called "The World of George Best". Someone on the programme said Best was the greatest but I said, "He won't be the greatest until he's been playing at least ten years. You can't say he's the greatest yet."

Just after that Best had a very lean time. He is a great player, there's no doubt about that, but I know two of the old-timers who were certainly as skilful – Bobby Irvine, the old Everton inside forward, and Peter Doherty.

Doherty was as good if not better than Best. The trouble with George is that he would run himself into trouble. There were times when there'd be a team-mate waiting for a pass, but he would go on and try to beat another man.

Talking about internationals, it always amuses me to read about the preparations the England team has before a game. In my day we used to report at the hotel on the night before the match.

The F.A. Committee used to run the team and they were all amateurs. There was nobody there to tell us how to play or talk about tactics.

The trainer, usually Tom Whitaker of Arsenal in my time, was in charge of the boys but his main job before the game was to look after the food and the travel arrangements.

In the England dressing room just before an international the only thing anybody said was "Good luck". Nobody ever discussed tactics.

Chapter Twenty

The best Everton team I played in

The best Everton team I ever played in was that which had that wonderful run between 1930-1933. I would rate them better even than the Everton team that won the title just before the Second World War.

There used to be nine internationals in the side – Sagar, Cook, Creswell, White, Britton, Geldard, Dunn, Johnson and myself. The only two uncapped players were Stein and Thomson.

Towards the end of my career at Everton I was playing in the Central League team a lot and at one time we had nine internationals in the side. The best international side I ever played in was the England team that beat Scotland at Hampden Park in 1927.

The team was Brown (Sheffield Wednesday), Goodall (Huddersfield), Jones (Blackburn), Edwards (Leeds), Hill (Burnley), Bishop (Leicester), Hulme (Arsenal), George Brown (Huddersfield), myself, Rigby (Blackburn), Page (Burnley).

We beat Scotland at Hampden for the first time for 23 years that day and I'll never forget that particular match.

The greatest players I played with or against must start with Elisha Scott in goal.

At fullback I would put Warney Creswell as far and away the best. I played with him and against him and he was the cream of the lot. The halfback line I would name is the Everton trio of Cliff Britton, T.G. Jones and Joe Mercer. I never played against them but they were the greatest halfback line I ever played with.

I know that if the forwards lost the ball we didn't have to worry about it – those three between them would get the ball back to us.

One of the best centre halves I played against was David Meiklejohn of Glasgow Rangers and Scotland. He was a great player, very clean, who went on the left to play football and play football he did.

My best forwards would be Joe Hulme and David Jack of Arsenal, Hughie Gallagher, Alex Jones of Arsenal and either Billy Smith (Huddersfield), or Ted Vizard at outside left.

They were the best of my day, and if they were all playing together now they'd win the sweep every week.

I don't think the tactics of today are better than they were in my time.

People used to go to matches then and see great wingers playing for every team who raced down the left and put the ball over. You don't see it today.

Up to a few years ago, of course, Liverpool had a couple of good ones who played like this – Ian Callaghan and Peter Thompson. I only wish I could have played with these two lads. I'd have scored plenty of goals from them but you don't see wing play today as I knew it.

But I am sure that football would be improved today if they went back to that old style. Players in my time had a great deal of talent and I am sure they would have been able to show it today just as well with modern play and training.

They talk about George Best being the greatest. Well Everton had this Irish boy, Bobby Irvine, who could dribble the ball from one end of the field to the other and nobody could take it off him.

It is ridiculous to hear people say today that the old-time footballer wouldn't live with the modern-day player.

The best club team Everton used to play in their great days was Arsenal. Herbert Chapman built that side and they used to call it the Bank of England team because he'd borrowed the money to create the side.

I can't see a wing half today in the game anything like as good as Joe Mercer. When Joe went into the tackle he never missed the ball. It was almost as though he had a pair of dockers hooks attached to his feet because he would hook the ball away from an opponent – and it wasn't a foul either.

I can't see a better concise player in the game today than Cliff Britton was. When he sent the ball over he laid them on to the inch. Mercer and Britton were two of the great ones all right.

I rate Gordon Banks very high but he isn't as good as Elisha Scott. But one player I would have liked to be playing alongside me in those old days was Bobby Charlton. He must be one of the all time greats and if he'd have been playing in my day I'd have used him alongside myself.

I'd have scored a lot of goals from his work and Bobby would have scored a lot from me. All I wanted as a player was somebody who could kick the ball when I headed it down to them and Bobby can certainly hit a ball.

Generally speaking, I'm not very impressed with modern football. When you think that they can earn more than £100 a week (1971) and people have to pay six bob (30p) just to stand up to see them, we expect a lot more entertainment than we get today. The spectator goes there to see the ball going into the net, not just to watch a placid game of football. And football today will have to change its ideas to keep spectators interested. They'll have to start scoring goals again and the way to do this is to go back to the old style of having fast direct wingers who can cross the ball accurately.

Chapter Twenty-One

Derbies? If I was playing today I would silence "You'll Never Walk Alone"

I played more than 20 games against Liverpool, League and Cup, during my years at Everton. These were the best matches of all. Anybody with the feelings I had for Everton was always dying to get on the pitch and get at the Reds.

Some of my happiest moments were when I was scoring goals at the Kop End and I am sure that if I was playing today I would be able to quieten that "You'll Never Walk Alone."

My great Liverpool rival was, of course, Elisha Scott. But although we were enemies on the field we were quite different off it. We used to have a pint together now and again and the first thing Elisha would say to me was, "I received the aspirins all right."

I used to send him a tube of aspirins with a note telling him to have a good night's sleep because I'd be there tomorrow to score goals against him. We used to have many a good laugh over that.

Tiny Bradshaw was the Liverpool centre half against me in most of the derby matches but I remember one time he was off injured and Norman Lowe was his deputy. Norman was only a kid at the time and he'd been told that wherever I went he was to follow me and not leave me alone for a yard.

Norman did a real good job. He went everywhere with me and I didn't get much chance to beat him until a couple of minutes from the end.

Then Teddy Critchley went down the right wing with the ball. I moved across as though I was going to run with Teddy and Norman Lowe followed me. Suddenly I back pedalled, moved back into the middle and when Teddy crossed the ball, only about three feet off ground I flew through the air at it, met it with the head and the ball went in the far corner. We beat the Reds 1-0 with that goal and poor Norman got a dog's life but he had done a great job in my opinion in that match.

There was another famous occasion when we played Liverpool in the Cup at Goodison. I scored first and we were well on top until Jimmy Jackson, the half back, set up a goal for Gordon Hodgson to make it 1-1. They beat us 2-1 that day and that was one of the softest games I ever played for Everton. I got my own back the next year when I beat Elisha 3 times in 9 minutes and that kept the Kop quiet.

But those games are always great – not only for the players but also for the spectators. You can hear them groaning and arguing but that's all there is to it. There's no such things as flying bottles and fights with rivals because all these people, the Evertonians and the Liverpudlians, are related.

You'll find half of one family follow Liverpool and the other half Everton, so they're not going to start battering hell out of each other, not like some of these other spectators do up and down the country.

I think Liverpool and Everton fans are the greatest of the lot. They're like a great big family of football fans and I would put next the Newcastle United fans. They are very fair and if you play a bit of good football they appreciate it and show it.

Liverpool's Tiny Bradshaw was not only a very good player, he was a very clean player as well. In all the times I played against him he never used any of those sly little tricks that others did, like pulling you back by your shirt or shorts. Tiny went out to play football and let the best man win.

He was in one of the greatest Scottish teams of all times - the famous Blue Devils who beat England 5-1 at Wembley in 1928. I was in the England team that day but we didn't have a chance against the Scottish. The forwards were all small men – players like Hughie Gallagher, Jimmy Dunn, Alex James and Alan Morton. But they played a beautiful game and they got goals so easily. They still celebrate it up in Scotland every few years. I was invited there to the last function and I met all those old players once more and we had a real do.

They all got up to speak about the match and they asked me to make a bit of a speech. So I just reminded them, "Don't forget what happened in 1927." Of course, I got a bit of a clap for that.

I get a lot of invitations today to visit clubs on Merseyside and bring my collection of cups and medals along to show them. I don't refuse anybody because I try to help them. Recently I've been going out to that new housing estate, Cantril Farm. They run about 8 or 9 sides there for the boys.

It's good to see them and see how hard they play and particularly when I look at the faces when I present them with their medal or plaque or whatever it is.

I always take my schoolboy medals with me on these occasions and show them to these boys. When you see their faces you know you couldn't refuse their invitation to help them.

I've spotted quite a few good kids at Cantril Farm. There was one lad there, about 12 years old, who played centre half but he did everything, taking corners and everything else. I'm sure he'll make the grade some day.

But I don't go up to Goodison these days. Harry Catterick has got enough on his hands without wanting to see me.

Chapter Twenty-Two

Ten goals– and the best game ever

The greatest match I ever played in was the Cup replay at Goodison against Sunderland in 1934. A lot of people even to this day say it was the greatest match ever played in England but I wouldn't know about that.

We had drawn 1-1 at Sunderland on the previous Saturday. The pitch was foreign and had been covered in straw before the kick off. It was a tough, hard march and Jimmy Cunliffe got a goal which brought the replay to Goodison. His shot struck the ground before the goalkeeper and the pitch was so hard that the ball bounced over the goalkeeper into the net.

After the match, both sets of directors complained to the F.A. about the referee's handling of the match and asked for another referee for the replay.

The FA agreed and they appointed a man called Ernie Rincston. He was called the 'Sergeant Major' and he was a right sergeant major at that.

Before the toss-up at Goodison he said to me, "Dean, go and get your team", and ordered the same to the Sunderland captain.

I said, "What for?" He said, "Do as I tell you." So when all the 22 players were gathered around him in the middle of the field he said, "If one man of you 22 lifts a boot today I'll send the lot of you off." I remember that well because he really meant it. He would have done it as well. The Sunderland team played me very tight and it was the other lads who got the goals. My job was to go up and nod the ball to them to score. It was a tremendous match. I think it was Cunliffe who scored first and then they scored and then Geldard got the next and they equalised. We scored again and were leading 3-2 with only a minute to go. Bobby Gurney, the Sunderland centre forward hit an overhead kick from the edge of the penalty area. Ted Sagar had come out and the ball flew over his head into the net.

So that was extra time, with a 3-3 score. We scored again and just before half time of extra time they equalised. It was a good job Albert Geldard had the strength to run down that wing because he won us the match that day. He made the centre for that goal and he even scored one himself at the finish, so we finished up winning 6-4. We certainly knew we'd been playing when we came off that day.

The best game I've ever seen as a spectator was the World Cup Final in 1966 when England beat West Germany 4-2. I thought that was a really great game.

Earlier that year I'd been to Wembley to see Everton play Sheffield Wednesday in the Cup Final as a guest of the club. That was a very good game and Everton won because they kept their heads even though they were two goals down. Before the match I'd been on a TV programme with Eamonn Andrews. Derek Dooley, the old Sheffield Wednesday centre forward, who is now their manager, was also on the programme telling Eamonn how Wednesday were going to win. But my prediction was that Everton would win by a goal and they did.

Everton took their goals well that day and young Mike Trebilcock will never score another goal, never mind two, like he scored that day. He'll never hit a ball as true as he did then.

Although I believe that the best football is the direct sort we played at Everton in my day, I also admire what is called the Scottish type of football with sharp passing, the classical stuff.

The Blue Devils played like that and they were very fast with it as well.

The nearest Everton have come to that in recent years was when they won the Championship two seasons ago (1970). But I think it was very significant that most of their goals were scored off Morrissey, the only international type of winger they've got.

But they had a shocking season last winter and the only reason I can see for that is that they were doing so much chopping and changing. It strangles me today the way some of the transfers are over £100,000. A lot of them aren't worth anything like it. It seems to me the clubs are prepared to pay any money for people who can score goals and it makes me think that I scored more than 400 of them in my day.

Of all those goals the one goal I remember best was not one of the record-breakers but one I scored near the end of my career.

I was due to play in the Central League team that day but Tommy Lawton cried off and I was put into the first team at the last minute. We were playing Sunderland.

By that time I'd finished what I called my "running days". I had put on some weight and I'd slowed up a lot by them. But in the match I scored the goal I remember best of them all. I got this pass and took the ball to about 10 yards outside the penalty area. I thought, "I know they're going to catch me up, so here goes." I hit the ball with my right foot and it flew right into the far corner, right across Mapson, the Sunderland goalkeeper.

I didn't move from the spot where I'd hit the ball but I called old Harry Cook out and said, "Cut out that piece of turf and let me have it." It was all a joke of course but I knew I'd never score another goal as good as that again.

Chapter Twenty-Three

As a boy I slept with my blue shirt and dreamed of playing for Everton. Thanks for making my dream come true

Football was full of characters in my day – on and off the field. Two of the best were Scotsmen, both tall fellows, great players and great personalities.

Jimmy Dunn, the old Everton inside forward, and Hughie Gallagher were the men I remember best – they were good enough to have been comedians on the stage.

One of Jimmy's tricks when we were staying in some of the best hotels in London was to buy some fish and clip it underneath one of the tables in the dining room.

After a few days we'd be having breakfast and there'd be a terrible smell in the room with the waiters trying to find what the smell was and where it was coming from.

He was always up to some practical joke or other.

I only saw Hughie Gallagher do a trick against Liverpool that I have never seen anyone else do. He beat both full backs, drew Elisha Scott out of goal and took the ball right to the goal line.

He put his foot on it, turned his back on the Kop crowd and as they started to jeer and shout at him, he turned to look at them and then back-heeled the ball into the net.

He was a real cheeky-faced Charlie but he was also the best ball player I have ever seen.

He was better than Alex James because he could dribble the ball past so many opponents in such tight spaces. James played a far different game -

hanging around in open spaces and when the got the ball he could pass it so accurately that he'd open up the way for someone to score.

One of those great players was Cliff Bastin, another great one. I played with Cliff in the England team and I don't think many people knew that he was deaf. But often, when the whistle blew for a foul or offside, he'd keep running down the field with the ball, not having heard the whistle, with the rest of us walking the other way.

Another trick that Hughie Gallagher used to get up to always had us all laughing. As we were having a drink together, particularly near some dock, he would look for some sailors and say to them, "There'll be a large Scotch and a pack of cigarettes for anyone who can walk the furthest on their hands."

So up they'd get trying to walk as far as they could and before long all their money would be dropping out of their pockets.

When this happened, of course, there they were all down on their feet again pushing each other around scrabbling for their money and it was a right carry on. Hughie, knowing what would happen, had vanished from the scene because they were all looking for him.

There used to be what they called Football Sundays at a church in Walton over near Goodison Park. The vicar asked me to read the lesson there one Sunday so all they boys wanted to come along and hear how I got on.

Being Sunday lunchtime we'd had a few drinks before we went to the church and Johnny O'Donnell – what a character he was – told me he wanted to read the lesson. All the players stood in a group near the pulpit as Johnny got up to read the lesson. He started off, "I will now read the first three chapters of the book of Guinness."

Of course, all the lads got terribly embarrassed and started whispering to him, "Genesis, you dope, Genesis."

Everton transferred Johnny to Blackpool and at one time there was a real scare about him. Blackpool wanted him to play in a match but he was up in Iceland. He'd met a captain of a trawler at Fleetwood and just decided to go off with him for the trip.

I don't see any of my old teammates now. In fact the only one I've met for years was Cliff Britton. He was the only one of us who ever went into football management and he has had a wonderful career.

Cliff doesn't smoke or drink but whenever I met him his first words were, "What are you having, Bill, and what do your friends want?"

I've had some wonderful experiences in football and looking back I wouldn't want to change any part of my life if I had the chance.

I always had an ambition to play for Everton, even as a boy. I always wanted to play locally. I was glad to go to Tranmere because I knew I'd still be on Merseyside – and in a blue jersey.

To repeat, I had some wonderful experiences in football and wouldn't want to change any part of my life.

I always had the ambition to play for Everton as a boy. When I was a Laird Street School in Birkenhead, we wore blue jerseys and on the night before a match I would sleep in mine because it meant so much.

And I'd dream of playing in Everton blue. It was the dream that came true and I loved every minute.

Dixie Fact-File

• Born January 22, 1907 at 313 Laird Street, Birkenhead.

• Started playing for Laird Street School and Albert Industrial School before turning out for Wirral Railway and Pensby Institute.

• Joined Tranmere as an amateur in November 1923, turning professional the following April. In two seasons at Tranmere, the teenage Dean scored 27 goals in 30 league games and also played in three FA Cup ties without adding to his tally.

• Signed for Everton on Wednesday March 18, 1925. He scored 349 league goals in 399 appearances for the Blues and another 28 in 32 FA Cup games.

• While at Goodison, he also won 16 England caps, scoring 18 times and notched nine goals in six inter-league matches.

• After leaving Everton, he played in a dozen matches for Notts County and found the net three times giving him a career record of 440 goals in 497 games.

• In all those matches, he was never booked or sent-off.

• He hit 37 of his 43 career hat-tricks for Everton.

• He remains Everton's record scorer in Merseyside derbies with 19 goals in 17 outings against the Reds.

• He took 17 penalties for Everton, converting 11.

• Dixie's roll of honour included League Championships in 1927-28 and 1931-32, a Second Division Championship in 1930-31, an FA Cup in 1933 and two Charity Shields in 1928 and 1932.

Career Statistics

DIXIE'S SEASON-BY-SEASON EVERTON BREAKDOWN.

Season	LEAGUE App	Gls	FA CUP App	Gls	TOTALS App	Gls
1924-25	7	2	0	0	7	2
1925-26	38	32	2	1	40	33
1926-27	27	21	4	3	31	24
1927-28	39	60	2	3	41	63
1928-29	29	26	1	0	30	26
1929-30	25	23	2	2	27	25
1930-31	37	39	5	9	42	48
1931-32	38	45	1	1	39	46
1932-33	39	24	6	5	45	29
1933-34	12	9	0	0	12	9
1934-35	38	26	5	1	43	27
1935-36	29	17	0	0	29	17
1936-37	36	24	4	3	40	27
1937-38	5	1	0	0	5	1
Overall	**399**	**349**	**32**	**28**	**431**	**377**

Acknowledgements

All text in this book is the copyright of
Trinity Mirror/Liverpool Daily Post & Echo.

The majority of images are the copyright of
Trinity Mirror/Liverpool Daily Post & Echo.

Other agencies/ photographers include:
Gordon Whiting
Central Press Photographs
Sport & General Press Agency
Fyfe
Tom Scott
W. Cull

We have used all endeavours to trace sources although many agencies no
longer exist. The publishers would be pleased to hear from anyone whose
copyright has been unintentionally infringed.

Other Everton Publications

If You Know Your History (with Breedon Books)
Everton's Z-Stars
Official Everton Annual 2005